INNOCENCE LOST

Joni Stuart

TABLE OF CONTENTS

PROLOGUE

For me, writing is a spiritual journey – a revealing of my soul. What is my soul?

My soul is my inner most being put there by God at conception. My soul is the essence of who I am. It is my connection to the universe. It is my connection to mankind. It is my reflection of God. It is God in me, the Holy Spirit. It is everything good and sacred.

Life lured me away and I traveled far from my soul. I became buried beneath the rubble of worldly pleasures, desires, tragedies and confusion. I was lost. Under the weight of guilt, fear, doubt and low self-esteem, I wondered if I would ever be found. One night in anguish, I cried out to God. Hearing my cry, he spoke to me. With every fiber of my being, I knew it was Him.

I listened. Slowly, following His guidance, piece by piece, I began peeling back the layers of rubble. Often painful, often uncovering what I didn't want to see or revisit, I persevered.

God laid it on my heart to write and with no concept of where that would lead, I obeyed.

Through writing, I began to catch glimpses of something beautiful buried within me. Glimpses of God's deep love, enduring hope and eternal connection. With this, I was propelled to dig deeper, search wider and write more.

I began to realize these glimpses of beauty were glimpses of the soul that was embedded in me by God in the beginning. All that is good. All that is perfect. I came to understand that God has always been in me, always by my side, day or night. I cherish these glimpses of what is truly good and perfect.

But, I'm still human. As long as I'm alive, I'll never be able to peel away everything, and may even pile bits of rubble back on.

The good news is, that when those final layers fall away, I will be in heaven, basking in the revelation of God's glory in my eternal home.

CHAPTER 1

LIFE THREAT

It was 1972, and my first summer in Palm Desert, California. I had been warned about the hundred-degree daytime temperatures, but they didn't bother me and I loved the balmy nights.

Looking over at our towheaded toddlers playing on the floor, I smiled with joy. Two girls in two years was a surprise, but never once had I felt overwhelmed or burdened. Tracy and Melissa were my sweet, sweet blessings.

I glanced at the clock, 6:15, my husband, Pat should be coming through the door any minute. The aroma of simmering spaghetti sauce filled the air. It was Pat's favorite. I hummed a tune as I reflected on the reassuring phone call just a couple of hours earlier.

"Just checking on what's for dinner?"

"Spaghetti," I replied.

"Sounds great, see you around six."

Last week, fighting back tears, I had finally mustered up the courage to let Pat know how important it was that he spend more time with me and the girls. I thought I was being reasonable, telling him it was okay to go to the bars on occasion. I understood he wanted time with his golf pro buddies, just not every night.

I checked the clock again, 6:30. I decided to give the girls a quick bath and get them ready for bed. They loved their baths and those squeaky-clean fresh smelling bodies in their cute little jammies melted my heart. The reality of motherhood had far surpassed my dreams.

Bath time transitioned to story time. The words of "Goodnight Moon" became blurred on the page. The voice inflections I usually interjected with enthusiasm when reading *"A quiet old lady who is whispering hush"* came out monotone and lifeless. Finishing the story, I tried to quell the all too familiar quiver starting in the pit of my stomach. I hugged them both extra tight as I kissed them goodnight. I shuffled to the kitchen with shoulders slouched.

The held back tears began to flow.

He was not coming.

Why did I always get my hopes up? I wished I could be angry, but I was just sad, sad that he could do this to me and to our daughters. I was doing all I could to provide a good home for our little family, but it didn't seem to matter to him.

The spaghetti sauce had thickened and started to become crusty around the edges. I boiled some pasta and heated enough garlic bread for both of us just in case. The anticipated savory meal was tasteless, my appetite gone. I felt nauseous and could hardly swallow through the lump in my throat.

As I prepared for bed the red, tear-stained puffy face looking back at me from the bathroom mirror was not my own. I paused and stared straight into the dull, lifeless eyes. "Where have you gone wrong?" I asked myself. "What have you done to make him treat us this way?"

I lay down on the couch and hugged my knees to my chest.

The Johnny Carson show was on TV, but the jokes and silliness I usually chuckled at went unnoticed. As usual, the test pattern came on at midnight signaling the end of programming for the day. I went to bed only to lie awake in the dark. My heart felt heavy.

In the early morning hours, I heard the all too familiar stumbling, bumbling sounds of my drunk husband entering our home. I pretended to be asleep hoping he wouldn't bother me for sex, but that seldom worked. How sad that the gentle, caring, lover I shared a bed with in Nebraska became a borderline rapist after a night out drinking in California. He could still be desirable when sober, but my ability to enjoy those times was eroding away.

This time he was hungry for food. Usually I would oblige him, but for some reason I meekly spoke up, "You should've been here at six when dinner was ready."

He grabbed me by my arms and pulled me out of bed. A tennis player and golfer I was fit at 5' 4" and 125 pounds, but no match for him at 6' 2" and 185 pounds. In a voice as cold as ice he threatened, "Fix me my spaghetti, now!"

He shoved me roughly down the hallway toward the kitchen. I crouched down in fear, trying to focus. Behind me, he yanked open a drawer and pulled out a large butcher knife. Spinning me around, he violently shoved me up against the wall and with his hand at my throat snarled, "I could kill you right now."

I turned my head to the side as the butcher knife blade passed near my face with enough force to penetrate and stick in the wall behind.

"See how easy that would be? Now fix me my fucking dinner."

With trembling hands, I pulled out the pots and pans, reheated the food and put it out on a plate.

He staggered over to the table, picked up the plate of food and hurled it across the room. The plate smashed against the wall near the ceiling. Spaghetti, sauce and bits of shattered plate began to slowly slide and drip toward the floor. He gathered up the pots and pans and jammed them into the clothes washer. The agitator hitting the metal pans filled the air with a dreadful clangor. All the while he was ranting, raving, swearing and threatening.

Out of the corner of my eye I saw movement. There stood Tracy bleary eyed and crying. Wild with fear, I rushed to her side.

Reeling from side to side Pat approached us and in the same menacing tone snarled, "You love this little girl, don't you?" As he spoke, he bent down, took her tiny little arm and twisted it behind her back, "I could break her arm so easily."

My heart leaped into my throat and I couldn't breathe. I snatched Tracy up, held her tight to my chest and carried her to her room. Through choked back tears, I assured her everything was okay praying she would go back to sleep. Miraculously, she stayed in her room.

With the loud clank, clank, clank of the washer in the background, desperate for help, I bolted out the front door. The gravel landscape cut at my bare feet as I raced to the neighbors. I

11

pounded on their door, expecting Pat to grab me from behind at any moment. I couldn't roust anyone.

Breathless, I kept running, down the street and around the corner. I glanced back to see if I was being followed, but I couldn't see much in the dark. Halfway down the next block a porch light was on. Through the window I saw the silhouette of someone sitting at a table. I leapt onto the porch and banged on the door. When a young man opened it, I fell into him and managed to blurt out, "Help me, help me, PLEASE! My husband just tried to kill me!"

An EMT on call, he stared down at me with a wide-eyed look of astonishment.

"Do you want me to call the police?"

"Yes!" I sobbed. "He's there alone with my babies."

Waiting for the police to arrive seemed like an eternity. Too much time had elapsed already. Frantic, I jumped into the back of the police car shouting directions and pleading with them to hurry. The two officers entered the house with guns drawn. I slipped in right behind them, my heart pounding.

Pat was sprawled out on the living room couch snoring loudly. I jostled past the officers to the girl's room. Thank God they were sleeping peacefully in their beds. I hurried to shut off the washer hoping there had been no permanent damage to the machine.

The officers put away their weapons. We sat down at the dining room table. Still breathing hard, flushed and shaking, it took me a few minutes to catch my breath.

They were patient, consoling and concerned. One of them began the process of writing up a police report. I answered the routine questions and described what had happened to the best of my ability. "Do you want to press charges?"

"What would that mean?"

"We'll take him with us and put him in jail."

I thought about that and what it would mean to our lives. What if he lost his job? What would I do then? It was too much for me to comprehend.

Before I could answer, the officer asked, "Are you going to be okay by yourself here with your children? Do you want to call someone to come be with you?"

With a deep sigh I replied, "I can't press charges."

Suddenly, my body felt as weak and limp as a rag doll. I wanted to go to sleep. "I don't need to call anyone. Once he passes out the crisis is always over."

They exchanged glances that said, we've heard this before. The interrogating officer gathered up the papers, and on his way out handed me a card and said, "If you change your mind give us a call."

I felt a twinge of guilt for wasting their time.

I dozed off only to be wakened by the sound of the shower at six a.m. Slowly the ugliness of the night came creeping into my consciousness. Fear and loathing consumed me. What should I say to him? What will he say to me? How do we even start a conversation? My body was tense and I couldn't focus.

Suddenly Tracy and Melissa appeared at the doorway.

Giggling and laughing they climbed into my bed snuggling close, one on each side of me. I wrapped my arms around them drinking in their warmth and innocence. Without them I wouldn't have had the strength to get out of bed. They scampered ahead of me to the kitchen where I busied myself fixing them breakfast.

Any apprehension I felt about having to talk to Pat was unfounded. He came walking down the hall, dressed for work and left the house without saying a word. I was grateful there was no confrontation, but at the same time appalled he could just go about his day as if nothing had happened.

I desperately needed help. I wanted to cry out to God, the God I used to know. But we were estranged. I had disobeyed Him years ago and was unworthy. Furthermore, He had allowed tragedy into my life in the past and I couldn't forgive Him. Yet, I knew in my heart my girls were a blessing from God. *Maybe I could go to Him.*

What I didn't know yet, was I was already carrying our third child.

CHAPTER 2

SUNDAYS AND CHURCH

I was born prematurely to Gordon and Rosemary Lane on September 25, 1945. Weighing in at 5 pounds 15 ½ ounces, I spent the first few days of my existence in an incubator. There were already three children in the family, two girls, Carol, age 6, Becky, age 5 and a boy David, age two. We lived at 1822 Avenue G in a tiny two bedroom house adjacent to my paternal grandmother's larger house. When I was four years old, we moved into a modest two-story red brick house built by my step grandfather at 2023 Avenue E. Just after I turned five, my little brother Bobby was born.

My idyllic hometown, Fort Madison, Iowa, was a town of approximately 20,000 residents situated in the southeast corner of the state along the Mississippi River. The small downtown area, consisting of just a few blocks, was near the east end with two movie theaters, the State and the Fox, on opposite sides of the street from one another.

Central Park, adjacent to the downtown area, covered four square blocks with a white bandstand in the center where musicians would gather to play on special holidays. On summer weekends the park would be filled with families picnicking, children playing on the playground and impromptu games played on the vast expanse of green grass under giant oak trees that kept the area cool on muggy days. There was even a pond full of goldfish. The town's claims to fame were the Iowa State Penitentiary, the Swing Span Bridge that connected us to Illinois, the Santa Fe Railroad that provided the livelihood for many of the men in town and the Sheaffer Pen Company, where my dad worked.

On every corner of the town square there was a church of a different denomination. From my earliest memory our family of seven rose early to attend the First Christian Church on Sunday mornings. Dad's trick to wake us up was to turn up the volume of Tennessee Ernie Ford belting out gospel music. "*On a hill far away stood an old rugged cross,*" came wafting up the stairs. If that wasn't enough to roust us, then the glorious aroma of bacon frying would do the trick. Dad was in charge of breakfast so mom could have time for herself. He cooked rows of bacon and pancakes on a black iron griddle. David, sat next to me giving me a teasing punch now and then while Carol and Becky, chatted away about school and friends. Little Bobby sat at the end of the table in his highchair. The five of us would eat as fast as dad could cook.

With tummies full, up the stairs we'd go as mom came down the stairs to prepare the noon meal.

"You girls help Joni get dressed," she said in passing.

Putting an apron on, mom browned chicken in a skillet and put it in a roasting pan or maybe it was a pot roast with carrots and potatoes to be cooking in the oven while we were at church.

My two older sisters wore the same size clothes and would argue about who would wear what as they helped me get dressed in my Sunday best dress with black patent leather shoes that pinched my feet.

"Joni, come here, let me brush your hair," Becky smiled. I sat real still savoring the attention from Becky. Her touch was gentle and loving. "Your hair just doesn't want to behave does it? She laughed.

Dad would come to the bottom of the stairs and holler up, "No dilly-dallying, the bus is leaving at 8:45," as the gospel music continued to play in the background. The seven of us would pile into our grey Plymouth sedan and off we'd go.

I liked Sunday school and learning the Bible stories with the help of flannel boards depicting the various characters. The church service followed Sunday school, so we were at church for at least three hours.

My parents didn't just attend church they were part of the backbone of the church and deeply involved. They each taught a Sunday school class. Dad was a deacon and also on the Elder Board. When a building committee was formed for adding on to the church, dad chaired that committee. He had a strong tenor voice and sang in a barbershop quartet as well as the church choir. He would even fill in with a sermon once in a while when the pastor had to be away. Dad once told me he wanted to be a preacher and was sorry he didn't pursue that path.

Mom was a deaconess and served many years as church treasurer. Each Sunday she brought home the offering in a large burgundy drawstring bag. After the noon meal she would dump all the money out on the dining room table. Many members pledged a certain amount of money to the church at the beginning of the year and each week put a portion of their pledge in a special envelope. There might be different envelopes for the building fund drive or other special need and it all had to be documented in one big ledger.

When I was old enough, she let me help. While mom documented the designated giving, I would organize the loose bills and change. She patiently taught me how to put the coins in rolls without dropping them or having them turn sideways in the roll. I took pride in the task, but the best part was spending special time with mom.

Every Wednesday night we attended a family night potluck supper at the church.

Once a month, on Thursday nights, mom hosted church circle meetings at our house. She would always prepare a special dessert to serve the ladies.

However, even with all of this church involvement, religion didn't permeate our family life. We didn't have family worship time, or reading of scripture. Our prayers were simple and quick, reserved for supper and bedtime.

The year I turned eight, along with five of my classmates, I dutifully took the series of classes the church offered designed to prepare a child to make the decision to commit their life to God. The ten-week session ended with a baptism ceremony in front of the congregation.

Baptism was by immersion and the baptismal was a cement enclosure behind the front wall of the sanctuary with steps at each end for entering and exiting the water. There were curtains on the front side that were drawn open on baptism Sundays.

It felt strange to be wearing my bathing suit under the church issued white smock. As I entered the cool water it took my breath away. The smock billowed up with air as I descended the stairs. By the time I reached the floor of the baptismal the water was up to my shoulders and the smock was puffed up under my chin causing a floating sensation.

Pastor Ives took my hand to steady me as I took a couple of steps toward the center of the baptismal, Then, with one hand raised in the air and one hand supporting my back he recited, "I now baptize you, Joan Lane, in the name of the Father, and of the Son and of the Holy Ghost."

He had a handkerchief in the raised hand and placed it over my nose and mouth. I instinctively placed my hands over his as he cradled my body in his arm and leaned me backwards until I was completely immersed. He quickly lifted me back up to a standing position and made sure I had my balance before releasing me.

My water soaked white smock was heavy and drippy as I made my way up the steps. In the bathroom, shivering from the cold I stripped naked as mom wrapped a big fuzzy towel around me and hugged me tight whispering, "Good job honey."

Afterwards at the reception, lines of adults came up to congratulate me. Some shook my hand and others hugged me. The women's big bosoms would press into my face and I could smell the men's cigarette breath as they spoke.

In the afterglow, I felt a sense of pride that I had done the right thing. Yet, I was a bit disappointed. I expected to feel some sort of miraculous transforming zap from God, but that never happened. I wondered if any of the others who got baptized felt anything and thought about asking my friend, John, but was afraid he might say yes. This left a slight doubt in my mind and a tiny question that maybe my baptism didn't take.

CHAPTER 3

THE FARM

Sunday nights were special. The atmosphere was relaxed, we sat casually around the kitchen table laughing and talking while dad popped popcorn in a pan on the stove. Dad grew this special Japanese hull less popcorn on the farm and the salted, buttered kernels melted in your mouth. This was the one night of the week we were allowed to drink pop instead of milk. The hardest part was choosing from the variety of Coca Cola, Root Beer, Nehi flavors, Dr. Pepper and 7-Up. Mom would take her bowl of popcorn into the living room while she read the Sunday paper and worked the crossword puzzle.

We lived in town, but when I was nine, Dad purchased eighty acres of land about three miles outside of town from one of his distant relatives. In the beginning he had grandiose thoughts of planting crops to sell. He proceeded to plant a large field of soybeans with the aid of Bud Hoenig, a neighboring farmer. Once the soybeans began to grow so did the gnarly weeds. He enlisted all of us kids to be his farm hands but the weeds were gigantic and impossible for us to yank out of the ground. Dad soon realized he couldn't farm and hold down his nine to five accounting job at Sheaffer Pen, so he leased out the lower fields to Bud.

There was a small one bedroom house on the property that I played in and pretended was my own. It had artesian wells with one pump in the front yard and one over the kitchen sink. In order to get water out of the spout the pump had to be primed. I liked pumping and drinking the well water. It was safe to drink, but had a metallic, musty taste to it. I was sad when dad rented the house out to an elderly man and I couldn't go over there anymore.

Across the road from the house was dad's garden. Dad grew way too much of everything, with rows and rows of corn, tomatoes, strawberries, peas, green beans, squash – anything that was in season. Mom wasn't always aware of what dad might be bringing home with him on any given trip to the farm. She might find herself immersed in stemming strawberries or snapping beans unexpectedly at the end of her day, but she never complained.

The farm was dad's refuge and my playground. We would often go there together, just the two of us but it wasn't always just to play. One cold, early March day he asked, "Joni do you want to go with me and help plant peas?"

"Yes," I replied eagerly.

"Okay, but it's getting late so we have to hurry or we'll run out of daylight. Get your warm jacket, mittens and boots it's cold out there."

When we got there, dad pounded stakes in the cold hard ground with a sledgehammer to mark the ends of each row. Then, he tied string around one stake and stretched it taunt to the stake at the other end. He had a hard time pounding in the stakes because the ground was still frozen. He showed me how to hollow out a hole for each seed a few inches apart right along the string line. I had to drop one seed into each hole and cover it with dirt. I couldn't manipulate this chore with my mittens on, so I took them off. The soil was like ice! My fingers became numb and tingly and my hands ached. The sun was setting and the evening chill was so cold we could see our breath in the air. We finished the job by the light of the headlights of the car. On the ride home, my hands ached from the cold, but it was worth it to spend the time with dad.

During the month of August, dad would monitor the ripening of the corn. Then, he would declare to the entire family what Saturday we would be expected to be there all day to help, no excuses. He would go out to the farm at the break of dawn and pick the corn. He brought it in on a rickety slat board trailer he hooked to the Plymouth. The trailer had wooden sides and he filled it as high as the sides would allow. He backed the trailer up to the back stoop of the house. Our back door opened directly into the kitchen. He and David stood in the trailer husking the corn and throwing the ears onto the linoleum floor. Two of us were stationed at the kitchen sink to remove the silks and trim the ends of the ears, preparing them for blanching. Mom had every burner of the stove going with large pots of water boiling, but only so many ears could be cooking at one time. The corn was boiled for just a few minutes and then plunged into containers of cold water. The next step was to cut the blanched corn off the cobs with a sharp butcher knife. As the kernels of corn fell off the cobs into a milky pile, someone else had to be ready to scoop up the corn and put it in plastic baggies.

The sealed bags were then transferred to a large open crate. Once the container was full of bags, they were taken to the basement and transferred to the freezer. If you got tired doing one job you could rotate to a different job, but there was no leaving until the task was completed and the kitchen cleaned up. The floor became a slippery, milky mess by the end of the day. We had no air conditioning and the sweat would drip off of us in the hot muggy August heat.

Even after canning and freezing there was always excess. We kids would take our little red wagon around the neighborhood distributing produce. Families were always glad to participate in the harvest and it warmed my heart to hear their appreciative comments about how there was just something special about what came out of Gordon's garden. The sweet corn and tomatoes were sweeter and juicier, the strawberries were lush and red with no sugar needed!

There was an old dilapidated barn on the property that at one time was vibrant with activity, but by the time dad bought it, that barn was run-down and deserted. For David and me, it was the ideal place to play cowboys and Indians. We spent many a summer afternoon in and around that old barn. The barn had a hayloft with leftover bales and loose hay strewn about. There was a rope with a pulley hanging from the rafters, perfect for swinging on and landing in the soft hay. The various stalls on ground level were ideal for hitching up our pretend horses or hiding from the enemy. We would gallop around the grounds surrounding the barn on our imaginary horses pretending we were the Lone Ranger, Gene Autry or Roy Rogers. Oh, how I wished I had a real horse! Dad was always worried we'd get hurt, but that never crossed our minds.

In the hills above the barn was an old cemetery where many of my ancestors were buried. I was always a bit apprehensive about going in among the broken down tombstones, but the epitaphs were still visible and fun to read.

Another lure on the farm was the tractor. It was an old tractor even then, a 2N Ford model, grey and red in color. When I was small, dad would let me ride up in the seat with him. Then, when I got big enough to reach the pedals and gears, he taught me how to drive it. Once I learned how, he would even let me drive it by myself.

I shared in dad's love of this property, and until teenage friends and school activities interfered, I spent many carefree hours there. Being outdoors in the open countryside was much more appealing than helping with household chores at home.

In the fall we would take hikes in the woods. Sometimes dad would take his gun and shoot squirrels and rabbits that mom would fix for dinner. Other times we would gather black walnuts in buckets from the many trees on the property. Black walnuts have a green husk on the outside that needs to be removed before you get to the nut itself, so dad would do this messy job because the husks stained your skin and clothes a sickly green. Then, he put the walnuts in a gunnysack. On snowy winter evenings, dad and I would sit down in the basement with that huge gunnysack between us. He would pull the walnuts out of the sack one at a time and break them open with a hammer, because the shells were so hard and stubborn you couldn't use a regular nutcracker. Then, we would take a nut pick and pry the nutmeats out of the pieces of shell. The nutmeats were so hard to get out of those black walnuts. I had to be very careful I didn't get any shells in the bowl of the nutmeats. It was a tedious, painstaking endeavor, but the black walnut cake mom made out of it was well worth the effort.

Each Christmas, the family would trek through the snow to find just the right size tree for decorating. Dad would lug his chain saw up the hill, and deep in the woods, would cut down the tree. We would all help drag the tree back to the car.

The pond was a source of activity throughout the year, but my favorite time was ice skating on it in the winter. The pond was small enough that it froze completely over several inches deep. Dad would monitor the weather conditions and know when the surface was right for ice skating and hockey games. When we had a big snow storm, we would have to first shovel the snow off and then sweep it with a broom to get down to the good ice. If the water happened to freeze while it was snowing, the ice would have a really rough surface. The best ice was after the first really hard freeze and before it snowed.

On one of our Saturday afternoons alone at the farm together dad stopped what he was doing and said, "Joni come with me I want to show you something." Taking my hand, he helped me navigate the steep incline above the pond. We climbed for several minutes and about halfway up the hill he stopped. "Okay, turn around," he commanded.

In a voice filled with excitement and enthusiasm he exclaimed, "Look at this view. I want to build a house right on this spot with a big picture window. See way off in the distance? That's the main highway to Montrose."

I squinted my eyes and could make out the cars, looking like ants traveling along the road. It was a pretty view, with the pond in front and nothing but farmland between us and the highway.

He continued, "This is God's country out here away from the hustle and bustle of town. Your mom and I could retire here once you kids are all grown and out of the house." I couldn't fathom living there, but understood, and relished sharing this special moment with dad.

Unfortunately, life got in the way of his dream. Financially, a college education for his children took priority. However, the biggest stumbling block may have been mom. She wasn't too keen on being way out there with no immediate neighbors. She liked the convenience and security of town.

CHAPTER 4

BECKY

From the time I was five, I shared a large bedroom with my two older sisters, Carol and Becky. They slept together in a double bed with my single bed tucked in the corner on the other side of the room.

As teenagers they were close, sharing clothes and chores, giggling about boyfriends and school, lifeguarding in the summer, being camp counselors, competing at ping pong in the basement, bickering at times and helping care for their three younger siblings. I wasn't privy to much of their world and often felt like the pesky little sister they wanted out of the way.

I was in awe of Becky with her thick brown hair and green eyes. At 5'11" she was a statuesque beauty and sometimes appeared aloof, perhaps even a bit snobbish. She had a long graceful neck and was given the nickname of "Swan." One of my friends referred to her as Fort Madison's version of the girl from Ipanema, "*Tall and tan and young and lovely. . .* "

In the fall of 1958, Becky enrolled at Drake University in Des Moines, Iowa, where Carol was already attending. Dad knew the dean of the school and wanted all of his children to graduate from Drake. Becky's high school sweetheart, Hal Moore, enrolled there too. Through high school she was the beauty and he was the athlete. They were a handsome couple. Hal was an extrovert and spent many hours at our house. I liked it when he came over because he paid attention to me and made me feel important.

After a month at Drake, Hal drove Becky down and dropped her off at our house to spend the weekend with us while he visited his family. On Sunday afternoon, Becky waited for Hal to pick her up and take her back to school. He never arrived. In the confusion that followed, she learned he was with another woman. Clearly, he had stood her up. I'll never forget the heartbroken sobs coming from behind our closed bedroom door. That very night, Dad hastily arranged to drive her the three hours back to Des Moines himself. I felt her sorrow, too, because I really liked Hal.

After the breakup, Becky had many suiters, but I sensed she never got over Hal. Her senior year of college she met Irv Geller. Irv, a Canadian, four years older than Becky, was Jewish by birth. While they were dating he visited our home on several occasions. As a professed atheist, he didn't believe a family like ours existed. I questioned his upbringing because he never talked about his family. I didn't like the way he often mocked our families' traditions, closeness and caring for one another.

Late one night, I was alone watching TV in the living room with all the lights out. Irv came quietly into the room, and as I glanced over at him he slowly took off his shirt. I was startled, but didn't say anything. Then, he began assuming different flexed poses as if he were in a body building competition. My eyes widened in disbelief. Then, he got down on the floor between me and the television set and began counting as he did a hundred push-ups. I sat frozen on the couch. I never liked him, but now I didn't trust him.

Becky graduated from Drake in June of 1962 and she and Irv married in September. It was a small wedding in the chapel of our church in Fort Madison. She was a stunning bride in a short white dress with cap sleeves that looked more like a sundress than wedding dress. Her veil was simple and she carried a small bouquet of white flowers. No one from Irv's family attended the wedding.

Following the family tradition, in my senior year of high school, I reluctantly applied for college at Drake. Once accepted I cringed with dread each time I saw the Drake postmark on another letter. It seemed like every few days there was news about my dorm assignment, roommate, jobs, sororities and on and on. From the time I was twelve, I babysat for various families and pretended their children were mine, dreaming of the day I could have children of my own. I wanted to stay home, get married and have babies. Dad, on the other hand, reacted to each communication with excitement at the thought of his fourth child attending Drake University.

As expected, college life wasn't for me. I never felt settled in my dorm and I longed for the security, comfort and familiarity of home not to mention how much I pined for my boyfriend, Roger. One night, I called home hysterically sobbing and begged dad to let me drop out of school. We finally came to an agreement that I would finish one semester and if I still wanted to drop out, then I could.

Fortunately, Becky and Irv lived a couple blocks away in married student housing. Becky had already graduated and was teaching fifth grade, but Irv was finishing his final year at Drake. Even though he was four years older, his stint in the military had put him behind. Spending time with Becky was my only refuge. I began to know her as a person and not just my older sister. She became my friend and confidant.

My attempt to join a sorority was a fiasco. I felt so humiliated and it all seemed so fake. All those gushy dressed up, made up women with their insincere chatter and snobbish demeanor made me sick to my stomach. I didn't care whether they liked me or not, and wasn't about to fake it to be like them. I was supposed to go to six houses, but after the first one, I turned around in the middle of the street and walked back to my dorm.

The following afternoon after class, I stopped by Becky's apartment. She immediately sensed something was wrong. She put her arm around me and said, "What's up?"

With reluctance, I shared my sorority experience with her, thinking she would be critical of me. Instead she started laughing. "Oh Joni, we should've talked about this beforehand. I feel the same way about sororities, that's why I never joined one." She gave me a big hug, and at once I felt good about my decision.

A few days later, I confessed to Becky about my sobbing phone call, begging dad to let me come home. Chuckling, she smiled and said, "Remember your first year at Camp Lookout?"

I thought back to the time when I was eight and went away to camp for the first time. I was so homesick. Both of my sisters were even there as counselors of the camp and I couldn't be consoled. The only way I got through the first night was to talk to mom on the phone with the assurance she would come get me in the morning. I got through the next day and by the end of the week I cried and cried because I didn't want to leave my newfound friends.

I half smiled and said, "Yeah, you're right."

Becky said, "Believe me, I understand about Roger, too." Tears welled up in her eyes. "It was so hard for me when Hal and I broke up."

In addition to my personal struggles, our country was in turmoil. On November 22, 1963. President Kennedy was shot. That afternoon, Becky and I sat in her living room in shock, not able to believe what we were seeing on TV.

I spent at least three evenings a week at their place while Irv was at football practice. Becky and I would often try to solve the problems of the world as we prepared dinner for ourselves. Becky and Irv were sympathetic to the civil rights movement and talked about going down south and participating in the marches. She and I talked about how dangerous that could be as Peter Paul and Mary sang *"If I had a Hammer. . ."* on the phonograph in the background.

One particularly blustery Wednesday afternoon, as I was scurrying toward their apartment to get out of the cold, I swore I saw dad. He was bundled up in his trench coat, hat and gloves as he quickly got into his car and drove away. *How could that be? It was the middle of the week.*

Slipping and sliding up to their door, "Becky, was that dad?" I blurted out, as the wind whipped the door shut behind me.

She was at the kitchen sink with her back to me.

"Yes." I could barely hear her reply.

"What was he doing here? Why didn't he come see me?" I could see she had been crying and I went over and put my arm around her. "What's wrong?"

"Irv and I are having some problems." She said softly.

"What kind of problems?" I asked as we sat down on the couch next to each other.

"I found out he's having an affair." Her tears began to flow.

"Oh, Becky, I'm so sorry. I've seen him sitting in the cafeteria with this very pretty girl, but never thought he might be cheating on you."

"I don't want you to worry, Joni." She said, wiping her eyes as she tried to compose herself. "We're trying to work things out. He promised me, in front of dad, that he wouldn't see her again. For now, I have to believe him."

Poor Becky. After what she went through with Hal and now this.

Five months later, on a gorgeous spring day in May I was at home in Fort Madison having fulfilled my end of the bargain to stay in school one semester. Mom was outside watering her newly planted pansies when I arrived home from my newfound job. We stood together talking in the warm sun anticipating the arrival of Irv and Becky. They were coming for the weekend to help celebrate grandma's 25th wedding anniversary.

We heard the telephone ring and mom handed me the hose while she went to answer it. When she didn't come back right away, I turned off the water and went inside. Mom was sitting very still by the phone staring off in space.

"Who was that?" I asked, a bit concerned because of the blank look on her face. She didn't respond right away.

"Uh, it was someone. . . from the highway patrol," she stammered.

"Why is the highway patrol calling here?"

Again, she didn't respond immediately continuing to stare off into space. "There's been an accident. . . on Dead Man's Curve."

I knew Dead Man's Curve well. Every time we made the trip back and forth from Fort Madison to Des Moines, we had to maneuver that stretch of highway and always talked about how dangerous it was.

In a flat monotone voice Mom said, "Becky is dead."

Suddenly my heart started racing. "No, Mom, wait." I ran over to her, knelt down, taking her hands in mine. "There has to be some mistake. Becky and Irv will be coming through the door any minute now."

I was frantic inside, *this can't be true.*

Then our eyes locked and the sadness I saw there pierced my soul.

Still trying to convince myself and her, I said, "They wouldn't tell you something like that over the phone, would they?"

That very moment the doorbell rang. Mom slowly rose out of her chair and made her way to the front door.

My subconscious was shouting. Don't answer the door. If you don't answer the door we don't have to learn the truth.

"Are you Mrs. Lane?"

"Yes."

"May we come in?"

Without speaking she stepped back while the officers entered our home and sat down at the dining room table.

"We have some bad news." One of the officers spoke. "Your daughter Becky was involved in a car accident in Mt. Pleasant. If you don't mind, I would like to read from the report."

Mom whispered, "Go ahead."

"Mr. Irv Geller was driving his 1964 Volkswagen south when it went out of control on Dead Man's Curve near the Ray Elmore farm home." The officer paused for a moment speaking softly, "Are you familiar with that area?"

Mom gave a slight nod.

The officer took a deep breath. Pain distorted his face as he leaned forward placing his elbows on his knees with the paperwork in front of him. It was all he could do to continue reading. "The car slammed into the cement abutment at the bottom of the hill on the passenger side. The force of the impact spun the car around and it hit the abutment on the other side of the road, again on the passenger side. The first people at the scene found Mrs. Geller partially inside the car with her head outside. Mrs. Geller died at the scene. Mr. Geller was taken to Henry County Memorial Hospital in Mt. Pleasant in satisfactory condition with a head injury, scrapes and bruises."

All of the feeling left my body. Inside I shouted, No. No. No. No. No. No. No. No. Not Becky. Please No. No. No. No. No.

My brain stopped thinking. Everything went dark.

I must have fallen asleep in my room, because the next thing I heard was dad calling for me. "Joni, Joni we need you to come down here."

Still groggy and a bit disoriented I made my way down the stairs. Mom and dad were by the front door.

"We need to go to Barr's to discuss the funeral arrangements. You and Bob need to answer the phone while we're gone."

"Can't we just let the phone ring until you get back?" I pleaded.

"No, we're waiting to hear from your Aunt Goldie with information on when her train arrives. She's spending tomorrow night here. Make sure you write it down," Dad said tersely.

"But we don't know what to tell people." I choked.

"Joni, this is no time to argue, people need to know what happened and information about the funeral in case they want to come. I've written the details down on that tablet by the phone. We'll try not to be too long." Mom and dad walked out the door.

While mom and dad were gone, the phone rang constantly. The minute one call ended the phone would ring again. Repeating the details and listening to the reaction of friends and loved ones on the other end of the line was excruciating.

The next morning, Saturday, mom and dad were either absent or isolated, mourning in private. I had nowhere to turn, no one to talk to. People were in and out of the house all day offering their condolences, bringing food and helping out. I couldn't go downstairs without being confronted with a well-meaning "How are you doing, Joni?" or "Have something to eat, you need to eat." So, I stayed in my room. I wanted them out. I wanted to be left alone.

Irv was released from the hospital, and arrived at the house Sunday morning, making matters worse. He went around the house wailing and sobbing. He kept repeating, "I'm sorry, I'm so sorry."

He'd come right up to my face demanding a response. I had no words to speak, but inside was screaming, Shut up! Shut up! This is our precious Becky. You have no right to go around acting like she means more to you than to us.

Knowing how I felt inside I marveled at the strength of my dad. Mom isolated herself in the bedroom, but dad was doing what he could to try to console Irv. I don't know how dad held it together. With the knowledge of Irv's infidelity, what he was dealing with now would test any man's ability to cope.

I had overheard mom and dad discussing their desire to have an open casket for the visitation and funeral. Because of the damage that had been done to Becky's neck and face, the undertaker was having difficulty treating her with cosmetics for display. I couldn't bear to listen. I couldn't get the image of Becky, her chest crushed and her beautiful swan neck broken, out of my head.

In the dark of that night, I stared up at the ceiling asking, "Why God why? We're a good, God-fearing, Bible believing family. You're supposed to protect us."

If I had stayed in school, I would have been riding in that car with them. Maybe I'd be dead too. I'd rather be dead.

These thoughts swirled around in my brain as the hours slowly ticked by. I wanted this all to be a nightmare, a bad dream that I could wake up from and shake off. But it wasn't.

My few experiences with death had been elderly or sick relatives and though sad, it never affected my faith. God was still great and good. Passages from the Bible and the knowledge that loved ones would meet again in heaven someday eased heartache and loss. This was all well and good for them, but not for my Becky.

Now, no scripture could ease the ache in my heart.

Where was this great God of love and comfort?

Thank goodness I had Roger.

CHAPTER 5

ROGER

The summer after sixth grade was my last as an innocent carefree child. Junior High was a big adjustment for me. The confidence and security I felt in grade school, among friends I had known since kindergarten, was now challenged. I had gained weight over the summer and for the first time was conscious of my appearance.

During the second week of school, just before my twelfth birthday, I began having my monthly periods. I was confused and bewildered. No one had ever talked to me about this, so when it happened, I was clueless. For the first four days I went to school with a discharge in my underwear and thought I was dying of internal bleeding. Mom noticed when she was doing the laundry and had my older sister explain to me what I needed to do and showed me where everything was kept. We used belts and safety pins to keep the pads in place. I had heavy periods that lasted for a full seven days and would completely soak through any pad in a short period of time. I couldn't get them changed fast enough. I was always having accidents. I would get physically sick on the first day of my period each month with migraine headaches, horrendous cramps and nausea to the point of throwing up. Mom would have to come get me or bring me a change of clothes.

I felt inferior to many of the girls who came from the wealthier families on the east side. Many of them were attractive and seemed unapproachable with their confidence and poise. In my first year of junior high, seventh grade, we had a girls' only homeroom class at the start of each school day. Mrs. Alexander, our advisor, worked hard at encouraging us to intermingle. I was invited to slumber parties at different girl's homes and even convinced mom to let me have one at our house. By eighth grade my circle of friends had grown, but I was still intimidated by a few of the elite, including Kelly Green.

I was surprised, yet excited, when Kelly invited me to her fourteenth birthday party. I had never been to her upscale house and my knees felt weak as I walked up to the door. As I entered the house I was struck by the high ceilings and lavish furnishings.

In honor of Kelly being born on St. Patrick's Day, green and white shamrocks and four-leaf clovers adorned the snack table with green fruit punch to drink. In the center of the table was a cake with white icing and green trim with Happy Birthday Kelly in bright green letters.

She must have invited the entire eighth grade. There were kids everywhere. I hesitantly joined a cluster of girls huddled together chatting, giggling and whispering about the boys on the other side of the room. Thankfully, a few of them were familiar friends and my comfort level began to rise.

Lively music was playing from the record player and a few of the girls began fast dancing with each other, but the boys were too shy. Towards the end of the evening, in her attempt to get the boys and girls to mingle, Kelly put on a Johnny Mathis album, turned the lights down low and announced, "Everybody find a partner."

"Wanna dance?"

I looked up and Roger, a boy I had never met, was standing in front of me.

"Do you wanna dance?" He repeated and held out his hand.

I had never danced with a boy before. I took his hand and followed him to the middle of the room. Our first few dance steps were awkward and rigid, neither of us quite knowing what to do.

"Walk my way and a thousand violins begin to play…"

Soon we fell into a dreamy rhythm, holding each other close. My heart skipped a beat.

"But it might be the sound of your hello, that music I hear, I get Misty the moment you're near."

The song ended, the lights were turned up and we just stood

there holding hands.

The next day, Roger called and we talked until dad came by and said the twenty minute time limit was up. We continued to talk until he came by again with a harsh reminder.

The phone was only to be used for necessity and short periods of time because we were on a party line. Sometimes we could hear the click of someone on the party line trying to use the phone, and on more than one occasion a voice would say, "Hang up, I need to use the phone."

At school we looked for each other at lunch, between classes and after school. We were smitten, always hand in hand, gazing into each other's eyes and stealing a kiss whenever possible.

Roger lived a couple of miles away and walked to my house and back even on the coldest of nights. He became one of the family, at our house every weekend. He ate meals with us. He joined in on the monopoly games, card games and family night activities. We double dated with my older brother David and his girlfriend.

A few months after the St. Patrick's Day party, we were passionately making out on the couch. It was way past my bedtime.

"Roger, it's so late. You need to go." I said, trying to sound firm.

"Just a little longer."

The euphoria I felt when we kissed so passionately was intoxicating. I felt so safe and secure in his arms. "I don't want you to go," I whispered after another passionate kiss, "But I'll be in big trouble if dad finds out you were here this late."

Reluctantly, we untangled ourselves from each other and made our way to the front door.

"I love you," I whispered in his ear after one last kiss.

Thinking he was heading out the door, I turned away. Instead, he came up behind me and lowered me to the floor. I lost my virginity, at the age of fourteen.

Roger, the last child in a family of ten, lived in a big house on the poor side of town. His dad was retired from the railroad and not well. I didn't know what was wrong with him, but the atmosphere at their house was dark and somber. We seldom went there, both of us preferring to be at my house.

His married sister, Karen, lived on the outskirts of town. They were a fun couple with a new baby and would often have us babysit. This was the ideal setting for Roger and me because once we got the baby to sleep we had the house to ourselves.

Roger's family didn't attend church, but he was a good person, shy and soft spoken. He didn't use bad language or drink like so many of the other boys. He excelled athletically in football and wrestling. I was the devoted girlfriend, cheering him on at every contest.

He worked at the Hy-Vee grocery store as a bag boy, and saved enough money to buy a dilapidated two-tone green clunker Mustang with a damaged front grille and floorboard you could see through to the street. It was parked in front of our house every weekend.

On warm summer nights, we would drive to an old abandoned trestle bridge down by the railroad yard and make out as the moonlight streamed through the car window. We were in our own little world and in love.

My ninth grade Sunday school teacher, Mrs. Erickson, was a skinny, mousy little woman with horn-rimmed glasses. Her class consisted of six ornery boys and me. She was more flustered than usual this Sunday because we were studying 1 Corinthians 7 and the boys were all giggly and squirmy as the subject matter was sex. Mrs. Erikson hurriedly read through the passage and simply stated, "Sex outside of marriage is a sin."

My friend, John, Roger's best friend, caught my eye from across the room and snickered.

Wait. I was confused. *How could our intimacy be a sin?* Roger was always sweet and caring. We loved each other. *Didn't my baptism protect me from sin?*

Yet, there it was in scripture. I had sinned against God. A sense of shame and unworthiness washed over me.

It never crossed my mind that I should stop having sex with Roger, but from that time on I suppressed my guilt. On the way to choir practice in the car with dad, I was no longer my usual chatty uninhibited self. Standing next to dad on Sunday mornings belting out "Holy, Holy, Holy" the guilt intensified, knowing Roger and I had had sex the night before.

I began having vivid nightmares. In one recurring dream I was out by the alley burning the trash in our incinerator and a man came riding toward me on a bicycle. I became frightened and started running. I looked back over my shoulder and he was always just a short distance behind me.

My legs felt like they were in quicksand. I would run but get nowhere. As the dream progressed, I was in an abandoned building with many vacant rooms where I would try to hide, but he was always there. I would be jolted awake by the sensation that I was falling down a staircase or falling out a window trying to escape.

My worst nightmare I only dreamed once, but it haunted me forever. My mother came at me with a knife and started cutting me into little pieces. "I'm so sorry, Joni, but I have to do this because you have been such a bad girl."

I awoke sobbing uncontrollably.

Mom heard my cries and came into my room to console me. She sat down on the side of the bed and began to gently rub my back. "Did you have one of your nightmares?" She whispered.

I was sobbing so hard I could barely nod my head.

"Sometimes it helps to talk about your dreams, then they don't seem so scary." She offered.

There was no way I could tell her what I had just dreamed.

She continued to rub my back and speak calming words in

her soft loving voice, and I drifted back to sleep.

How could I lift this burden of sin off me? Abstinence wasn't an option. When Roger's father died during our senior year of high school, he didn't talk much about it, but I could feel his emotion through the intensity of our lovemaking. I was there for him, and it brought us closer together than ever. I rationalized, as long as we married someday everything would be okay.

Somehow, I had the ability to separate my guilt from my involvement in high school. I participated in many activities and enjoyed them all. I was assistant leader of the Kilties, a girl's marching drill team. As an athletic tomboy, I was president of the Girls Recreation Association. I was president of the Future Teachers of America and assistant editor of the yearbook.

My junior year of high school, mom went to work for a local accountant. With no one at home, it made it easy for Roger and I to sneak home, have sex in my bed upstairs with just enough time to get back for the after school activities. Roger and I had no desire to drink and turned down invitations to the beer parties, content to be with each other. Ironically, I was labeled a goody-goody.

My senior year, I was nominated to be on the homecoming queen court. It was a tradition that the Letterman's Club, made up of all male athletes that lettered in any sport, to nominate the candidates. Roger was a member, having lettered in several sports, and after their meeting he excitedly told me I was one of the five girls nominated. He then told me the names of the other four candidates and none of the most popular girls were on the list. I asked him what was up. He told me the guys just wanted to give other girls, besides the most popular, a chance for some recognition. I actually won the election and became homecoming queen. It was quite an honor, but I couldn't help feeling like a second-string queen.

While I was at Drake, Roger was still living with his mother and commuting daily to a Community College nearby. Longing to be together we made plans for Roger to visit.

He came up on a Saturday and had to be back the same night. *Where could we go for some privacy?* We decided to get a hotel room in the middle of the day. We had to pick somewhere we wouldn't be seen, so decided on downtown Des Moines. He didn't have much money, so we ended up at an old seedy hotel in a sleazy part of town. Roger went in alone and registered. If the clerk as much as suspected any hanky-panky, we could be kicked out or maybe even reported to the authorities. We couldn't walk in together, so Roger came out to the car and gave me the room number and went back inside.

The ancient lobby was small, quaint and dark. It took my eyes a minute to adjust. Even the clerk was old. I waited until his back was turned, then, snuck past and started up the wide rickety stairs. The floorboards creaked, and I expected him to call out to me at any moment, but I made it to the room without confrontation.

We spent the afternoon making love and professing our undying love for each other. I told him about the deal I made with dad. When nightfall came, and Roger had to get me back to my dorm before curfew, the ache in my heart was unbearable.

"Joni, we have to go. You know how much trouble you'll be in if I don't get you back there. They'll lock the doors on you. I don't want you to have to go through that."

"But, can't we just run away? I don't want to go back there." My eyes were glistening with tears and he kissed them away.

"Just think, honey, it's already October and the semester will be over in December. It won't be long and you'll be back home again."

Those two months seemed to drag by, but I kept my end of the bargain and dad kept his. At the end of the semester I was back home in Fort Madison.

Amidst the upheaval and grief surrounding the tragedy of Becky's death just a few months later, I clung to Roger for some sense of normalcy, some sense of security. I needed him, and the sooner we could get married the better. We settled on a wedding date the following August, when Roger would transfer from the Junior College to Western Illinois University in Macomb, Illinois.

For the next year, my job and the planning and preparation of our wedding helped suppress my sorrow.

Four different groups of friends and relatives hosted showers for us.

The sweet little lady from down the street who was sewing my wedding dress called me over for several fittings.

Invitations were decided upon, ordered and sent out.

Roger and I went for counseling sessions required by the church.

Mom and I decided on the menu for the reception to be held in the church basement.

On August 14, 1965, surrounded by friends and family, we were married by the same pastor who baptized me.

We honeymooned in Niagara Falls. While we were gone, mom and dad took all of our wedding gifts to our apartment on campus at Western Illinois University so we could go directly there upon our return. With my clerical skills, I secured a job at the Men's Physical Education building to support us while Roger finished his education.

I had finally atoned for my sin, and my happily ever after had begun, or so I thought.

CHAPTER 6

PARENTS ACCIDENT

Roger and I had been married over a year and my parents and brother were traveling the forty-five minutes from Fort Madison to Macomb after church on Sunday to visit us. My younger brother, Bob, was sixteen and proud to be officially driving with mom and dad safely buckled in the back seat reading the Sunday paper.

As I busied about, making sure the apartment was neat and tidy, I could hear the rain pounding on the roof.

They were late. This was unusual, as dad was always very punctual and took pride in being on time. The rain must have slowed them down. My biggest concern was the meatloaf in the oven. It was dad's favorite and I wanted it to be just right.

Two hours past the expected arrival time, I knew something was wrong. When the phone rang, I prayed it was dad with some logical explanation, but it was the local hospital. There had been an accident. We should come right away.

No, not another accident.

As soon as we entered the lobby of our small local hospital, I saw Bob and rushed over to him. "Oh my gosh, Bob, what happened?"

He held up his hand to keep me from hugging him. "My chest is really sore, but they took x-rays and my sternum is just badly bruised."

"What about mom and dad?"

"They've both been admitted to the hospital." My heart sank. "They're conscious," he said with a scared look in his eyes. "They have internal injuries. They're running tests now."

"Can I see them?"

"Yes, come on, they're right down the hall."

We went into dad's room first. Seeing him in that hospital bed was a shock, but I did my best to keep my emotions under control. I couldn't hug him because of all the paraphernalia surrounding him, so I just squeezed his hand.

"How are you doing?" I asked.

"Oh, Joni, I'm in some pain, but not too bad. They say I have a severed colon and they'll need to operate right away."

I glanced over at Bob to see how he was taking this news.

"How's your mother?" Dad asked.

Even though I didn't want to say those words, I came right out and said, "I haven't seen her yet, but Bob says she has some internal injuries too."

"Maybe we'll be in surgery together," dad quipped, trying to make light of the situation.

"I'll go see her now and then come back." I couldn't wait any longer to assure myself mom was okay.

When I entered the room, mom's eyes were closed, and I thought she might be sleeping, but she sensed my presence and her eyelids fluttered open. Those dark brown eyes always full of life and energy were now full of pain.

"Hi mom," I managed.

"Oh, Joni, look what's happened."

I leaned over and kissed her forehead, not knowing what to say next.

"Have you seen your dad yet?"

"Yes, he has internal injuries and the doctors are going to operate on him right away." Her eyes became anxious. Maybe I said too much.

A nurse came in and asked me to leave the room for a few minutes while they attended to mom.

Bob was in the hall, and we walked to the waiting room together. He had a personality much like dad's and was always very factual and logical thinking, even at the age of sixteen.

"What happened?" I asked again.

"Well, from what I can remember, it was raining really hard and I was going slow because the windshield wipers couldn't keep up and it was hard to see. All of a sudden, this station wagon appeared in my lane. Joni, I had no time to do anything but slam on the brakes

74

and hold on tight. We must have hit head on." He paused, as if reliving the moment, before continuing. "I believe mom and dad lost consciousness for a period of time, I'm not sure. But, when I asked if they were all right, they both said, no. Mom had hit her head on the back of the front seat, and I could see she was badly bruised. The rest is all a bit hazy, but the state patrol arrived, and I waited in the back of the patrol car while ambulances and wreckers cleared the scene. A state trooper gave me a ride to the hospital."

"Wow, you poor thing," was all I could say.

"I told you mom has internal injuries, but she also has a broken back and the doctors have her under observation."

A shiver ran through me. A broken back, that's serious. At least they are still alive.

On the morning of the third day, the decision was made to transfer mom to Iowa City where they could deal better with her broken back.

From that point forward, life as I knew it changed. Mom

became the focal point of my life.

Mom and I flew by medical helicopter to Iowa City. As we were leaving, her doctor handed me an 8 x 10 manila envelope instructing me to give it to the doctor at the other end right away, as it contained his findings and recommendations regarding her internal injuries.

The ride was uneventful and within the hour, mom was being wheeled into the hospital on a gurney, with me by her side dutifully clasping the envelope. When introduced to Dr. Green, I handed the envelope to him relieved to be rid of that responsibility.

Assigned to a room, the nurses made mom as comfortable as possible and she had dozed off. I had settled into a chair in the corner of the room and was reading a Jacqueline Suzanne romance novel, "The Valley of the Dolls."

Suddenly, there was a flurry of activity. Nurses and doctors came from everywhere. Someone announced, "She needs to be taken to surgery immediately."

The next thing I knew she was being wheeled out of the room. No one told me anything. All I could do was wait. Enough hours had passed that I finished the book I had just started that day. It had grown dark outside.

A nurse came into the room and said, "Gather your things, the doctor wants to see you."

My mouth went dry and I swallowed hard, because that meant we wouldn't be going back to the room.

The hospital in Iowa City was enormous with many floors and wings going in every direction. The doctor's offices were in the basement of the hospital down a lengthy, winding corridor with a maze of twists and turns. My legs felt weak and I was shivering from the cold and fear. I had no idea where I was going or what I would be told once I got there. Passing door after door, about to give up, I finally came to the one labeled Dr. Green. He was sitting at his desk, and as I cautiously entered the room, he stood up and put out his hand to greet me. We shook hands.

"Sit down," he said gesturing toward the chair on the opposite side of his desk. "What was your name again?"

"Joni."

"Oh yes, Joni. Are you alone?"

"Yes."

"Joni, I'll try to explain this as simply as I can. Your mother has internal injuries and a broken back. Because of the delay in dealing with the internal injuries gangrene set in."

What is gangrene? I wondered.

"As a result, I had to remove several inches of her intestine to make sure we got all of the damaged tissue. In order for the incisions to heal, she has to have a colostomy bag. If all goes well, this will only be temporary until her intestines can be reattached."

What was a colostomy bag?

He swiveled around in his chair and reached up for a plastic spine model that was sitting atop a file cabinet. "This is the area of her spine that is broken," he stated, pointing to one of the vertebrae. "However, I won't even begin to worry about her back injury at this point. She can't move anyway, and we need to get her internal injuries under control."

So far, he was being very factual and clinical.

Then he leaned forward, and staring with intensity straight into my eyes continued, "You need to know that none of what I have just described to you may matter. Your mother's condition is grave. The gangrene was advanced. We may not have been able to save her."

My eyes locked with his as he spoke again.

"You need to contact family members and let them know the severity of the situation. Every hour she lives is on our side, but it is that critical. There is a strong possibility she won't make it through the night."

Completely alone in a strange city, in a strange hospital, in the dark of night with this kind of news and no place to go, I began to cry.

Doctor Green came from behind the desk and put his arm around me. "I know how hard this must be for you. You can use my phone to make your calls, and I'll stay with you and talk to anyone who has questions for me. I can put you in touch with someone nearby who will rent you a room for the night."

A couple of hours later, after phone calls had been made and the lodging arranged I walked across the street with my few belongings to the big boardinghouse the Dr. recommended. My room was a small upstairs dormer room with a window. As I laid there unable to sleep, I could see the big full moon high in the sky and the lights of the city twinkling below.

I prayed, "Are you out there, God?"

I wanted an answer.

"God, if you're out there please help me. I thought I made things right by marrying Roger. Why did you let another tragedy happen to my family? You must not be there or else you wouldn't have let this happen."

The possibility that I might lose my mother, coupled with the possibility that God might not be real, was too much for me to comprehend. I closed my eyes and mind and slept fitfully for a few hours.

Mom's condition was touch and go for weeks. My sister, Carol, flew home from Germany where she was teaching. She took over the vigil during the week, while I went back to Macomb for work. Church friends who had recently moved to Iowa City offered their home to us. Carol was there full time, and I commuted and stayed with her every weekend.

At one point, mom had internal bleeding that couldn't be stopped. Dr. Green came to us and described a balloon procedure that he was going to try as a last resort. If that didn't work, he had no more answers.

That weekend, Dad was well enough to travel and came to visit. A group from our church caravanned to the hospital with dad. They formed a circle around mom's hospital bed and the pastor prayed over her.

Within a day or two the bleeding stopped. Was it the balloon procedure or God's answer to their prayers?

I wanted to believe it was God answering their prayers, but my faith was shattered. Why did this happen to her in the first place? I was still reeling from Becky's death just three short years ago. I thought my marriage meant something to God. Now this.

I decided it was the balloon procedure.

Mom began to improve ever so slowly.

The trauma of mom's ordeal took its toll on me emotionally. In my vulnerability, Danny Waskevich, the baseball coach at work, began wooing me. My life was already upside down and the attention of this outgoing, energetic sports figure was flattering. It was Christmas time, a year after mom's ordeal, and Roger was staying back in Fort Madison during his break from classes to work for the Santa Fe railroad. Danny called me at home one night, and asked if I would meet him. I did. We made out in the back seat of his car.

The following weekend, I went to Fort Madison for Christmas. Roger and I were staying the next couple of nights with my parents. Mom was given permission from her doctor to spend Christmas at home, so it was going to be a special time for us all. Roger and I were in the bedroom unpacking our things when he innocently asked, "I called you last Wednesday night but you didn't answer the phone. Where were you?"

His question caught me off guard and I blurted out the truth. "I was with Danny Waskevich." Roger knew full well he was the baseball coach from college.

He just stood there staring at me in wide-eyed disbelief.

"What do you mean you were with Danny?" His voice rose and his face turned red with anger as he spoke. I had never seen him angry before.

My tears began to flow and I couldn't speak.

Just then, dad called up the stairs, "Dinner's ready."

We somehow managed to compose ourselves through the meal. My brother, David, and his family were there, too. It was so good to have mom there after more than a year away. Everyone else at the table was upbeat and chatty. Our silence went unnoticed.

I was torn up inside. I didn't want to face Roger alone, so after the meal I went to the basement on the pretext of doing some laundry. Roger followed me down and we began arguing.

Suddenly, dad's booming voice rose above ours, "I don't know what's going on down there, but you two need to stop right now. We can hear every word you're saying. We're not going to let you spoil Christmas. Get up here now!"

The weeks that followed were a blur. I turned away from

Roger and became obsessed with Danny. I wanted out of my marriage.

Mom had been released from the hospital to recuperate at home before returning to the hospital for back surgery. I moved back home to help take care of her.

Dad was distraught about my affair and used every opportunity to try and talk me out of divorcing. He also forbade me to see Coach Danny while I was living under his roof. I felt like Hester Prynne in the Scarlet Letter, with a red letter "A" on my forehead.

After only being there for a week or so, he sat me down across from him in the living room. The same room where as a child we watched baseball together lying on the floor on humid Sunday afternoons rooting for his beloved Cubs. The same room where he made sure there was enough wood for the fireplace to last on a cold and stormy winter day. The same room where the family played games on a card table while the wind was howling outside. The same room where we sat in the late night together in his easy chair because neither of us could sleep. Oh, how I loved my dad.

With his Bible in hand, he began to speak. "Joni, if I can't get through to you maybe you'll listen to what God has to say." He opened the Bible and began reading.

"To the married I give this command: A wife must not separate from her husband."

I sat rigidly in my chair. *What about my sin of having sex with Roger when I was fourteen.* I was already doomed to spend eternity in Hell.

Dad continued reading, "And if a woman divorces her husband and marries another man she commits adultery."

Tears began streaming down my face. I still did not speak but wanted to shout, *where was God and your precious Bible when Becky died?*

He continued on, "By law, a married woman is bound to her husband as long as he is alive."

Where was God and your precious Bible during the car accident that put you in the hospital and almost took my mother's life? I couldn't listen any more. I walked out of the room, up the stairs to my bedroom and closed the door.

Dad had no idea of this fear of eternal hell I carried. Coupled with the intensity of my anger at God for taking away my sister and causing mom so much suffering I chose not to believe in God anymore.

It was the only way I could keep my sanity.

That very same week, I betrayed their trust by leaving mom alone for the day to rendezvous with Danny.

Dad wanted me out of the house and far away from this man. My brother and his wife offered that I could stay with them in northern Iowa, temporarily, until something could be figured out. A month or so later, my parents arranged for me to live with my mom's brother and his family in Lincoln, Nebraska, on the condition that I enroll at the University and pursue my teaching degree. I went along with this plan, because Danny told me not to worry. He would come for me soon.

I had been biding my time in Lincoln a few short weeks, when the eagerly anticipated letter arrived in the mail. I ran to my bedroom and closed the door. My hands trembled as I broke the seal of the envelope and hurriedly unfolded the single sheet of paper. My heart throbbed as my eyes devoured the page, searching for words of love and plans for our next rendezvous.

"You and I both know this relationship can't continue."

Huh? No.

My eyes blurred as I read the line a second time. "You and I both know this relationship can't continue." My arms went slack. I dropped the letter to the floor. I slumped onto the bed and began to sob huge heart wrenching sobs, burying my head in the pillow to muffle the sound. I wept for the betrayal of my lover, I wept for my destroyed marriage, I wept for my sister's death, I wept for my mother's ordeal, I wept until there were no more tears to weep. My ribs ached, my eyes were so puffy I could barely see, I couldn't breathe. I wanted to die.

For weeks I went around in a depressed fog. I attended class. I worked my part-time job. I shunned the attempts of my three young cousins to get to know me better.

My uncle arranged a date for me with the entertainment coordinator at the college. We went out a few times. Herb Alpert and the Tijuana Brass came to campus to perform and he took me back stage after the show to meet them all. That was exciting but he wasn't. He had pasty white skin, freckles and red hair. He had thin lips and a hooknose. He would try to kiss me and I would turn away.

I was broken. Beaten down.

I had a one-night stand with a diving coach that was in Lincoln for the National Diving Championships. Why not? Nothing mattered anymore.

Then, there was the handsome black college football star. The muscles on his body bulged to the point of bursting. He had these big soft kissable lips. My uncle saw us riding down the streets of Lincoln together. That night, he took me aside and forbid me to go out with him, because of how it would look for the family. I was shocked. My kind, soft-spoken, church-going loving uncle was racist! It was bad enough he was trying to control my behavior, but I couldn't accept his prejudice. I felt betrayed once again.

CHAPTER 7

FIRST MEETING

In March of 1969, I moved out of my uncle's house and began sharing a home with a married schoolteacher, Hilde Swensen, whose husband was away in the military. She encouraged me in my pursuit of a career in teaching. I began to enjoy my classes. I enrolled in summer school to make up for lost time and was beginning to settle into a routine.

With rent to pay, I had to supplement my part time job. A married college professor, John Williams, hired me to type his dissertation. He was attracted to me, flirtatious and fun, but he never did anything out of line. We enjoyed each other's company, and I did a good job for him. Vicariously, he was on the lookout for guys for me to date. During one work session, John gave me a coy sideways glance.

"Hey, Joni, on Saturday I was hanging out at the new golf course. You know, the one on the edge of town?"

I knew of it, only because it was just down the street from my uncle's house, but I knew nothing about golf. I nodded politely and kept on typing.

Eager to continue, he walked over closer to where I was working and leaned toward me.

"Well, the new pro is from California and he's looking for a decent looking woman to show him around town."

My fingers froze on the keyboard.

"I told him, I've got just the girl you need to meet."

Dad's words rang in my ears.

"Joni, you just need to focus on your education right now. That's what I've always wanted for you but you insisted on marriage to Roger. Then you had an affair and now you're divorced. I just don't understand it all, but you need to get your life back on track."

My Christian upbringing left no room for divorces and affairs. In fact, Dad had a hard time even saying those words. I felt like such a disappointment to my family and to myself. What was wrong with me? All I ever wanted was to get married, have babies and live happily ever after.

My thoughts were interrupted by the sound of John's voice.

"I figured you wouldn't mind and I gave him your phone number."

Why did I always take everything so seriously? Why not just go out and have some fun?

I agreed to a date with Pat McCormick over the phone, dinner at Tony & Luigi's, the best restaurant in town. I dressed and redressed asking my roommate which outfit was best. Why did I agree to go? I should have met him first. What if he was ugly, I couldn't spend the evening with an ugly man. Would he agree with John that I was a decent looking woman? I shouldn't be doing this. What time was it?

I opened the door to his knock and before me stood a tall, well-built, nice looking man with curly brown hair and a suntan. He was dressed in a suit and tie. Clutching at the neck of my cotton shirt, I immediately wanted to go change.

We were both uneasy on the drive to the restaurant and didn't talk much. I wondered what he was thinking. Was he nervous too? I had this urge to flee, but kept telling myself everything was going to be okay. At least he passed the looks test. I wondered if I passed his decent looking woman request?

As soon as we entered Tony & Luigi's I was impressed, and blurted out, "This is a nice restaurant, I've never been here."

He chuckled, "This is laughable compared to the restaurants in California."

It had taken courage for me to speak up and his response felt like a put down, yet I was curious about the restaurants in California.

A perky blonde waitress approached our table and began to introduce herself but Pat interrupted, "Hi sweetie, get us a drink, I'll have J&B rocks." He turned to me, "Joni what do you want?"

The only alcoholic drink I ever had, a Tom Collins, was to celebrate my twenty-first birthday. It was foul tasting and I couldn't finish it.

I looked up at the waitress and smiled, "What kind of soft drinks do you have?"

Pat gave me an incredulous stare, "Are you shitin' me? It's an Italian restaurant, you gotta at least have some red wine."

"Honey" he said to the waitress, "bring us a bottle of Mateus."

She returned with this cute little bottle of rose wine and poured me a glass. I managed to sip the wine along with gulps of water in between, wondering who was going to drink that whole bottle.

A relish tray was brought to the table when we were seated. After we ordered, the waitress brought crackers and spread. The meal came with soup, salad and a palate-cleansing scoop of lemon ice between courses. The sips of rose relaxed me a bit, and I began to enjoy myself. The salad was Caesar, mixed in a large wooden bowl tableside. My spaghetti and meatballs were delicious. I had never had a meal with so many courses. The rich red décor and low candlelight were very romantic.

Pat dominated the conversation, raving about his life in California. "La Quinta Country Club where I work, is closed for the summer, that's why I'm here. I can't wait to go back."

I questioned this in my mind, because I couldn't imagine a club not being open in the summer. But I didn't say anything. Whether or not his stories were true, he was an excellent story teller and I was impressed. I was happy to just sit and listen.

"The club is very private and exclusive with members like George Blanda, Chuck Knox, Clint Eastwood, Andy Williams, John Brodie, Frank Capra, Gerald Ford, Spiro Agnew and Governor Brown," he continued.

Some of the names I recognized and others I didn't, but it sounded very glamorous.

"Our club hosts the Bob Hope Classic each year. It's a pro-am and the best golfers in the world come here to play along with many celebrities."

I wasn't familiar with golf and didn't know what a pro-am was. I didn't recognize the names of the golfers he mentioned, but some of the celebrity names got my attention. I wouldn't mind meeting Clint Eastwood or Andy Williams.

"As golf pros, my buddy Davey and I can play any course in the desert for free. Davey is the best, you would really like him."

How does he know I would like him? He hardly knows me! I fantasized along with him trying to picture it all in my mind. California! It all sounded so alluring.

He ordered another JB rocks, took one sip and called the waitress over. "Sweetheart, this isn't J&B, take it back and tell the bartender J&B, not this cheap shit."

At the end of the meal he lit up a cigarette and offered me one.

"No thanks, I don't smoke," I said.

He gave me a friendly kiss goodnight at my door. His lips

were passable. I had mixed emotions.

Two days later, our next date started with drinks at the bar. I ordered my safe rose wine. I needed to eat if I was going to drink so we ate at the bar. Every stranger at the bar became Pat's friend by the time the evening was over.

The pleasure he derived from smoking and drinking was mesmerizing. He tapped his cigarette package a couple of times to release a cigarette. Pulling the cigarette from the package with his teeth he simultaneously extracted the lighter from of his pocket. One flick of the flame on the end of the cigarette was all it took. The first inhale was long and deep as if satisfying something deep down in his soul. The first exhale was equally long and strong. From that point forward the drags on the cigarette alternated with sips of the scotch. Not one for one. The scotch took precedence over the tobacco. The cigarette smoldered in the ashtray awaiting the next drag. I marveled at how much of the cigarette burned away in the ashtray as he drank and talked. The way he held the cigarette between his fingers and flicked off the ashes into the ashtray was theatrical. He was in a trance-like state as the alcohol and nicotine did their addicting work.

For the next week or so, we saw each other every night. Pat McCormick was unlike any man I had ever met. He had a crazy sense of humor and such a cavalier, devil-may-care attitude. The twelve-year age difference didn't seem to matter. He was an extrovert, and his stories were fun and exciting.

I had a hard time with his use of swear words and arrogant behavior. Not one man in my family or of my acquaintance growing up ever swore around me. The men I knew were kind and considerate. None of them drank. I knew that some of the boys in high school did, but I didn't associate with them.

One evening Pat got into a verbal fight with someone at the bar. The filthy language and demeaning, derogatory things he said to this total stranger made me cringe. I was embarrassed to be with him. I began to have second thoughts.

The next day I called him. "Pat, I don't think you're my type. I need to concentrate on school. I don't think we should see each other anymore."

"Fine, if that's the way you feel." He abruptly hung up the phone.

The trouble was, I missed his company. As foreign as some of his behavior was, we had fun together. I could let my hair down. I rationalized he was just angry and didn't mean the things he said that night at the bar, maybe I should give him another chance. He had given me a golf club to practice with at home, so a few days later I used this as an excuse and called him again.

"I still have your golf club and need to get it back to you," I offered.

He answered, "Keep it, I don't need it."

"I'm sorry I told you I didn't want to see you anymore, but

your behavior the other night was not nice. I was embarrassed to be with you."

"That guy was a fucking jerk, he deserved it."

"Well, I wish you wouldn't use that kind of language."

It would have been nice if he would have apologized, but instead he said, "Wanna go out tonight? My boss is in town and I'm meeting him for drinks at six. Why don't you come?"

"Okay, but I can't be out late, I have a final at 8:00 in the morning."

Dick Watson was about the same age as Pat. He was surprised to see me at the bar, and with a flirty grin plopped down beside me. The three of us talked, joked and laughed. I was flattered by the attention of these older men. I felt so young, beautiful and a bit sexy. I was glad I decided to join them.

I had never had hard liquor or mixed drinks, and the two of

them began suggesting drinks for me to try that taste good. The drinks had strange names like Black Russian, Screwdriver, Harvey Wallbanger and Tequila Sunrise. Before the night was over, I had tested five or six of these various potent drinks. I woke up on the cold tile floor of the bathroom in Pat's room at the Lincoln Hotel where he was living. I tried to stand up and I threw up.

With very little sleep and a pounding head I suddenly realized what time it was. "Pat, Pat, you need to drive me to campus and drop me off so I can take my final," I implored, shaking him awake.

He groggily muttered, "Don't worry it's just a test."

"But it's important to me."

"Then take the damn car."

I went in the clothes I was wearing the night before, reeking of alcohol, cigarette smoke and vomit.

I began spending nights with Pat at the Lincoln Hotel. How

odd to be living in a hotel. Walking through the front lobby I noticed two men in a dark corner sitting very close to one another and it looked like they were passionately kissing! I whispered with repulsion, "What are those two men doing?"

Pat laughed at my naivety and said, "Oh, it's just a couple of fags." This was my first introduction to homosexuality.

One night we were snuggled together sleeping soundly when suddenly he sat straight up in bed. He was visibly shaken, sweating profusely. When I asked what was wrong, he began to talk about his life in Florida.

"I was involved in racketeering and illegal gambling operations with a mafia figure by the name of Harlan Blackburn. I was his right hand man," he began.

He lit up a cigarette and the tip glowed red in the dark. "The FBI was out to get Blackburn and they approached me. Either I cooperate with them, or I go to prison too they threatened."

He took another drag on the cigarette.

"I made a deal to work with them and help them put Blackburn away. After many months of feeding inside information to the FBI, they had enough evidence to indict Blackburn. He is behind bars awaiting trial. The reason I left Florida was to escape the possibility of Blackburn retaliating in some manner."

In the silence he brought the cigarette to his lips once more.

I tried not to breathe or interrupt. I didn't understand much of what he was telling, but I knew this was something big. Part of me wanted him to stop, because I didn't like what I was hearing, but the other part of me wanted to hear the whole story. He sounded vulnerable and scared. I shivered and drew the covers up close to my chin.

"I don't know for sure when the trial will take place, but the FBI's keeping me informed. When they tell me it's time, I'll have to go to Florida and testify."

A chill ran through my body. Maybe someone was stalking us right now, ready to burst through the door and wipe us both out.

I was awake the rest of the night mulling all of this over.

He needed me to take care of him.

When summer classes were over, I spent my days at the golf course. Pat was responsible for every aspect of the operation. It was a small par three with only nine holes. The grounds needed to be cared for, as well as running the small pro shop. He taught me how to drive the fairway mower. The smell of the freshly mown grass dripping with dew in the early morning hours was a delight to my senses.

He started teaching me all about the golf business. I began ringing up the green fees and merchandise sales. The pro shop was stocked with basic items such as golf balls, gloves, tees and hats as well as snacks and non-alcoholic beverages. He worked with me on my golf swing. When we got bored, we livened things up by having sex in the bathroom.

Dinner out was the norm, but on occasion we frolicked through the grocery store hand in hand like teenagers, picking out something fun to fix in his little kitchenette.

On July 20, 1969 we watched Neil Armstrong take his *"one small step for man one giant step for mankind"* lying in bed together.

As the summer months waned, Pat started talking about having to leave for California. Sitting at his favorite bar sipping his favorite J& B rocks he turned to me and said, "Why don't you come with me?"

I couldn't believe what I heard. "Really?" I was giddy at the thought.

"Yes, I really want you to come."

What about dad, what about school and getting on with my life? "If I decide to go, you need to come to my sister's wedding next week, in Fort Madison, and meet my parents."

To my surprise, he agreed.

"But I can only be away from the job for a couple of days."

We traveled separately, as I was going to be there a week. I was nervous, yet, excited at the thought of sharing our plans with my parents, together.

Pat came for the wedding and spent one night sleeping on a cot set up for him in our unfinished basement. He left for Nebraska with no mention of our plans, leaving me to break the news alone.

Dad, mom and I were sitting around the kitchen table the day I was to leave.

"How were the summer school classes?" Dad asked.

"Fine, I got an A on my last final." *Hard to believe in my hungover state.*

"Have you decided on your classes for the fall?"

"Not yet," I took a deep breath, "Well, Pat wants me to go to California with him when he leaves next month and I'm going."

Abruptly Dad's voice raised a notch.

"What do you know about this man? You just met him. What about your education? You're just getting back on track, you seem to like school and are doing well. Oh Joni, don't throw this all

away again. After all everyone's done for you."

My decision to run off with a man twelve years my senior, I

had only known three months, was hard for my dad to accept, but

my mind was made up and I was going.

CHAPTER 8

CALIFORNIA

When October came, we loaded our few possessions, some clothes, his golf paraphernalia and our cat, Amy, into Pat's dark blue Thunderbird Grand Prix, so flashy compared to the practical sedans my family always owned. Pat was a cat lover and it was his idea to get this cute little Siamese kitten. I had never had a pet growing up and wasn't really into cats, but I grew to enjoy her antics as she frolicked around the golf course all day. Pets weren't allowed in the hotel, so we would have to sneak her in each night.

I felt so free as Lincoln, Nebraska disappeared from view. No more toeing the line, no more under the thumb of my dad or uncle. I was going far away from the burden of my past, away from the guilt and shame as the family outcast. Off to a new start in California with my new love.

I couldn't help but reminisce about our family's trip to California when I was eight. Our 1950's Plymouth Sedan had bench seats. Carol was fourteen, Becky was thirteen and David was ten. David and I took turns riding in the middle of the front seat. There were no seat belts and my feisty little three-year-old brother, Bobby, unable to be contained, was all over in the car. Dad drove and mom rode shotgun, with our luggage strapped to the top of the car with bungee cords. Dad had every aspect of our mid-summer trip scheduled with predetermined destinations. With no air conditioning, each day's drive began at 6:00 a.m. and ended at 3:00 p.m. The only stops were for gas, or a picnic lunch mom had prepared the night before.

A Best Western or Howard Johnson's motel with two adjoining rooms and rollaway beds was our usual choice, with a pool of course. We would burst out of the car like prisoners escaping, and start clamoring for our bathing suits. The evening fare was burgers, fries and chocolate malts.

Our ultimate goal was Dad's sister house in Barstow, California. We stayed with her family for a few days taking side trips to Knotts Berry Farm, Calico Ghost Town and of course the ocean. On our way to the coast we passed a large area of property under construction, and learned that Walt Disney was building a huge amusement park and going to call it Disneyland.

The first time I saw the Pacific Ocean, I thought my eyes were playing tricks on me. I could see it for a bit, and then it would disappear as we rounded a curve in the road. When it appeared again, it was a bit closer.

Standing at the water's edge, the vast expanse and sound of waves lapping at the shore frightened me. The unforgettable smell of ocean water, seaweed and sand filled my nostrils. I was lured toward the water, but at the same time petrified of getting any closer. The most I would do is put my feet in at the shallowest point. Back home in Iowa, I would often fantasize about California and that ocean, vowing someday I was going to go back there.

This was my someday, but I missed the happy family of seven from my youth. Both were gone forever.

Pat and I headed for San Francisco to visit a club member he knew, and drove the coastline down from there to Palm Desert, our final destination. Following State Route 1 through the Big Sur area was a sight I will never forget. Pat kept pointing out views to me, while trying to maneuver hairpin turns next to a sheer drop off into the ocean. I made him stop many times along the way, not only to drink in the magnificent scenery, but also to allow us to enjoy it together.

We arrived in Palm Springs late in the afternoon of the third day, and stopped at Johnny Banducci's Italian Restaurant for drinks at the bar. The bartender's face lit up with a huge grin as we entered. He came out from behind the bar and embraced Pat with a big bear hug.

"And who do we have here?"

His voice was flirtatious as his eyes undressed me. I flushed with embarrassment.

Pat laughed with glee as he relayed the story about Lincoln,

Nebraska and how we met. I wanted to feel proud, but the tone of their voices and their comments made me feel a bit trashy. After a couple of drinks, we said our goodbyes and moved on.

The same scenario took place several more times along the way, as we worked our way from bar to bar toward Palm Desert. I should have paced myself with the drinks. Feeling woozy, I was looking forward to eating and settling in for the night.

At each stop, Pat had asked, "Have you seen Davey?"

As we entered Palm Desert, Pat insisted, "We have to stop at Bash's because Davey will surely be there."

We pulled into the parking lot and Pat began shouting, "There he is, there he is!"

I looked in the direction where Pat was pointing, and saw a man sitting in a convertible. At least I thought he was sitting. Then, I realized he was standing by his car. Pat jumped out of the car with the motor running waving his arms and yelling, "Davey, Davey."

They hugged in an impassioned embrace, and strode arm in

arm into the bar with me following.

I tugged on Pat's sleeve and whispered, "I need food." He gave me a quizzical look as if he didn't recognize me, or as if to say, *Oh, are you still here?* He hastily dismissed me with, "You can order something at the bar," as he began carousing with everyone in the establishment. As additional patrons entered the restaurant they spied each other and the hugs and greetings started all over again. He was a local celebrity.

Several hours later, in the pitch dark, I heard muffled voices coming from somewhere. I tried to lift my head. A wave of nausea consumed me. I was lying on a bed with no bedding.

Where was I? Where was Pat?

I whimpered, "Pat . . . Pat."

Davey appeared in the doorway.

"Pat's right here, go back to sleep, we'll be back soon."

Then, I was out again.

The sound of loud Mexican music roused me from a deep

sleep. Warm sunlight streamed into the room. As I sat up, I was horrified to find that sometime during the night I had thrown up. There was vomit all over the mattress and all over me. My head pounded as I peered through the crack in the bedroom door. There was Davey, sitting at a small table in his tiny kitchen, smoking a cigarette, drinking a beer and gyrating to the lively music.

It took me most of the day to begin feeling like a human being again. I knew I should eat something, but the thought of food was repulsive. Pat found it quite amusing that I had a hangover.

"Where are we going to stay tonight? We can't spend another night here with Davey." I pleaded.

"Okay, we'll go over to the place I was living before I left for Nebraska. They'll have an apartment for us."

Fortunately, they had a one bedroom sparsely furnished apartment available and we could move right in. I was happy to have a place to call our own.

Pat had told me about his mother, Ann Dorsett, after a phone call he made to her while we were in Lincoln. Lying beside him as they talked I could hear most of the conversation. He kept rolling his eyes as he half- heartedly listened to her woes. She ended up crying before the conversation was over and I felt sorry for her.

He explained that she lived in Palm Desert too, but how their relationship had been strained for many years, ever since he found out she had adopted him at birth. The truth came out when he was twenty-five and travelled to Montana to attended his father's funeral. Someone asked Pat if anyone had ever told him about his dad. He learned bits and pieces through relatives at the memorial service and as he relayed all of this too me, I had a hard time following the sequence of things.

It seems, his mother, Ann, worked at a hospital in Montana where a woman gave birth out of wedlock, and couldn't keep the baby. Ann knew this woman's doctor and he knew Ann wanted to adopt a child so he arranged for Ann to take the baby. She was married at the time, but soon divorced. Ann remarried when Pat was a toddler and it was this man Pat had come to pay his respects to.

Finding out the man wasn't really his father, led to finding out Ann Dorsett wasn't really his mother. He wanted to learn more from her, but she would become hysterical whenever he tried to talk to her about it, insisting he was her baby. All of this left him feeling angry, confused and betrayed. He hated his mother for lying to him, but felt an obligation to her.

On our second day in Palm Desert, while smoking a cigarette and drinking his morning coffee, Pat nervously stated, "Well, let's get this over with, Joni, you need to meet my mother."

Ann Dorsett was a big, frumpy buxom woman. She wore a tiny print flowered mid-calf length dress. The dress came with a skinny belt, but it was only detectable from behind because it was hidden in the front by her big breasts laying on her bigger belly. Her shoes were black, boxy and clunky. She wore heavy nylons. Her glasses had coke bottle lenses with thick black frames. Her lips were quite thin and she smeared bright red lipstick on them. She was probably in her late fifties but looked seventy. I was apprehensive from the little I knew about her. The minute she opened the door, I could sense the neediness in her voice. She clung to Pat with tears in her eyes, "Oh, Pat, I've missed you so much."

As Pat attempted to introduce me to her, she looked right at me and abruptly stated, "Did he tell you about Patty? I don't think their divorce is final."

Was she deliberately trying to be cruel I wondered? In our conversations in Lincoln, Pat had told me about his ex-wife Maxine and about his two children from that marriage, but never anything about a woman named Patty.

Pat glared at her and quickly changed the subject.

That night, back at our apartment, reeling from this news, I sighed, "Pat, I'd better just go back to Nebraska and finish school."

He didn't answer.

Lying beside him in the dark, my father's questions haunted me. I really didn't know anything about this man. *Now what do I do? Go back with my tail between my legs? Admit to another bad decision? Go back where?*

I slept in, after a fit full night. When I awoke, Pat was sitting in our tiny living room watching television. "There you are," he said, when he saw me, trying to sound chipper.

I couldn't look at him. My head hurt and my whole body felt heavy from the weight of my dejection. Pat could sense my mood and knew I was wrestling with what to do.

"I know you're upset, Joni, but please don't do anything rash. My mother is just jealous, that's all. You'll get used to her. She wanted to make you think I'm still married, but I'm not. I'll make it up to you. Let's do something fun." He sounded desperate. "I know, we'll drive to Palm Springs and go up on the tram. It's an incredible experience. It'll cheer you up."

Still confused and upset by the news of this other woman, I did not want to go, but after some persuasion, I agreed. The trip began on the desert floor and as we ascended the scenery was breathtaking. The gondola swayed a bit as the cables and pulleys gently lifted us toward the summit. In a matter of minutes, we were transported from the stark desert wasteland to a winter wonderland of tall pines covered with snow. He took my hand as we strode over to the lookout point. In the winter cold, gazing through the tall pines to the hot desert floor below he began to speak.

"I'm going to tell you everything. You don't need to worry about Patty. There won't be any problems in that regard because she doesn't want to have anything to do with me."

He paced back and forth making crunching sounds in the snow.

"There's one more thing, we have a kid named Mark. He's

probably around two by now, but I haven't heard from her since before he was born. She vowed I would never be allowed to see the baby, she hates me."

He stared down at me with sadness in his eyes, letting that news sink in. "I understand if you want to go, but I love you and want you to stay. I promise things will be great."

My legs were weak, I needed to sit down. I became lightheaded. I felt faint.

Another woman was one thing, but an ex-wife and baby, that was another. Or, maybe not an ex, according to his mom. Were they still married? As astounding as all this was, I felt like I had no choice. Pat could have told me anything. The reality was, I couldn't go back. I had made my bed and I had to stay with Pat.

I began to spend time with Ann, and the more I got to know her, the sorrier I felt for her. She was needy and weepy, desperate for her son's love and attention that he wasn't about to give. She was widowed, and had been living alone for several years. She was constantly concerned about her health and would go from doctor to doctor getting medications prescribed for her imagined serious illnesses. If one doctor examined her and found nothing wrong, she would go elsewhere and seek another opinion. She didn't drive, and began to rely on me to take her where she needed to go. She had trouble getting in and out of the car, because of her size, and I would have to help her. She made no effort to help herself, so it was like trying to lift a dead weight. Doctor appointments led to picking up prescriptions and stops at the grocery store.

Interestingly enough, a non-drinker, within a short time of our arrival in October, she was diagnosed with cirrhosis of the liver. She rapidly became sicker and sicker. It was early December. We hadn't heard from her for over a week and I was concerned. "Pat, we should go check on your mother."

"If you're so fucking concerned about her you go."

The next day, I knocked on the door of her studio apartment. There was no answer. I knocked again. Nothing. I tried the door and it was locked. I tracked down the building superintendent and convinced him to unlock the door for me.

It took a minute for my eyes to adjust from the intense light of the desert sun to the total darkness of her apartment. Far back in the corner, I could make out her large form under the blankets of her single bed. The smell of rotting food, filth and decay overwhelmed me. Dirty clothes littered the floor, and I stumbled as I made my way to her bedside. Two beady eyes stared up at me like a trapped, scared animal. Her hair was matted to her head, and the closer I got to the bed, the stench of body odor, urine and feces caused me to retch. Her bedside table was filled to overflowing with pill bottles.

She was taken to the hospital by ambulance. Pat refused to visit her there. Within a week she was dead. I firmly believe she willed herself to her illness and death. She died of a broken heart, never having the love of her baby boy.

Pat returned to his assistant pro job at La Quinta Country Club. With the training I had at the par three, I was offered a job in the pro shop. A couple of weeks later, the club manager asked me if I wanted to take the receptionist position. It paid a bit more and would utilize my clerical skills, so I agreed. I began to meet and greet many of the rich and famous people Pat had talked about back in Lincoln.

Golf was the center of our lives. Each day more of the staff working for the various private clubs arrived in town. Some, like Pat, were returning for another season. Others were new hires in town for the first time. The bars were abuzz. Who was here, who was still coming? Who secured a year-round job and wasn't coming back?

I began to meet the wives and girlfriends. Our men catered to the wealthy by day and frequented the bars at night. Most of the women had left family and friends behind and were eager for female companionship. We grew tired of the bar scene and would gather at one apartment or another to talk about our lives.

We were a diverse group. Jeannie was a local dark-haired beauty whose boyfriend was a handsome golf pro from Wyoming. Rosemary, a tall, freckle-faced redhead, newly married, came from back east. She didn't like the desert and only lasted one season. Sheila, from Ohio, was in the desert as the nanny for a wealthy family and had hooked up with one of the golf pros.

Quite often, we ran into members at the local hangouts and they would buy us dinner or drinks or both. We had no money, but lived like we did. We gathered for impromptu parties. Many a night two or three guys would hang out in our tiny apartment, always with drinks in hand.

The golf bible of the day was Ben Hogan's "Five Lessons." They would get the book out, pull a golf club out of Pat's bag and in the middle of the room break down the stance, grip, takeaway, swing, and follow through. There were always "aha" moments when one of them swore they found the key. They would fantasize about how great they could be, if only they could swing like Ben. It was a carefree, fun lifestyle.

The first time a member invited us to their home for a private cocktail party, I was terrified. I had absolutely nothing in common with anyone there. Plus, it was a cocktail party, and I didn't like to drink.

The thought never crossed Pat's mind to stay by my side and introduce me to people to help me feel at ease. He was off with his J&B rocks.

A waitress with a large tray came up to me and asked, "What can I get you to drink, sweetie?"

"A screwdriver," I answered, just to have a drink in my hand.

The din of voices and laughter all around me only made me feel more out of place. Some gushy extrovert in an obscenely low-cut gown approached me with nosy questions. I gave her one-word answers, and she quickly moved on.

Pat breezed by and with a glare and tried to coax me into mingling.

A haze of smoke hung in the air from all the cigarettes. The women were dressed in elegant eveningwear, costing thousands of dollars more than whatever I managed to find suitable to wear in my limited wardrobe.

The party went on endlessly. When we finally departed and were alone in the car, I said, "That was unbearable. I was so uncomfortable all night long. Why did you leave me alone?"

Pat turned toward me, and in a menacing tone with bloodshot eyes and slurred speech snarled, "Then why don't you go back to fucking Iowa where you belong."

The next morning feeling very sorry for myself, I got a suitcase out of the closet and began filling it with my things. Pat walked into the room and asked, "What are you doing?"

"I don't want to be where I'm not wanted, so I'm leaving."

He gave me an astonished look, "Where did you get a crazy idea like that? Put that stuff away you're not going anywhere. I want you here with me."

Davey gave me golf lessons, and I became familiar with the terminologies and lingo of the golf world. It was a hard game to learn, but I was relatively coordinated and athletic so able to become somewhat proficient.

The joy of eighty-degree weather in November warmed my soul. Even the inexpensive apartment complex we could afford had its own pool. Pat was wrong. Fucking Iowa was not where I belonged. This was where I belonged.

The much-anticipated Bob Hope Classic came to the desert. Our club was one of the host courses. As the receptionist I greeted everyone who came through the front door. Touring pros were there for a practice round before the main event. I had come to know the names of many of the more prominent players and was excited to see them in person, even if it was for the brief moment they passed by my desk.

Some of our members were playing in the event, as well as entertainment and sports celebrities from around the world. On opening day, I gazed out the huge floor to ceiling windows of the clubhouse in awe of the vivid blue sky contrasted with the lush dark green grass of the golf course. Walking hand in hand towards me, down the middle of the fairway, was Andy Williams, his gorgeous wife Claudine Longet, and their two beautiful children.

After the round of golf each day, we attended parties held at various venues around the desert. Indian Wells Country Club was one of the most popular and many of the participants were there. What an experience to be partying with Arnold Palmer and Jack Nicklaus!

My glamorous job and newfound friends sustained me as I tolerated Pat's inebriation, late night hours and verbal abuses. I was learning to keep my mouth shut to avoid confrontation.

One morning in February, I woke up earlier than usual feeling a bit nauseated. I had not been out drinking the night before, so wondered if I might be coming down with something. A bite of food made me feel better, which seemed strange if I was getting sick. I didn't think any more about it and went about my day. The next day the same thing happened, and the next.

I shared this with a friend and she began to laugh.

"Why are you laughing?" I asked.

"Because I think you're pregnant, that's why," she chuckled.

WHOA. A visit to the doctor confirmed my friend was right.

Pat and I had never discussed marriage and children, but now we needed to. If we were going to have a baby, I wanted to be married.

To my relief he agreed. "Let's get married in Vegas," he said.

Getting married at the "Chapel of the Bells" on the Las

Vegas strip, amidst the circus atmosphere of lights, noise, people, gambling, prostitutes, shows, strip joints, cheap food, cigar and cigarette smoke, taxi's, hotels, nightlife, was the polar opposite of the atmosphere surrounding my marriage to Roger.

The chapel provided a driver to pick us up at our hotel. In the chapel we stood before a man dressed in a cheap, drab, ill-fitting suit, trying to make his voice sound like he really cared about us getting married. Canned music was playing in the background. Since it was just the two of us, the ceremony took place in a dingy, small side room of the chapel. There were sparse fake flowers on pedestals on each side of us making it feel more like a funeral than a wedding. I was excited, but melancholy at the same time. I missed my family, I missed my church, I missed my friends.

The ceremonial vows were boilerplate, sterile and short. We paid an extra five dollars each for cigar band type rings, symbolizing our love and commitment to one other. When it was over, I saw the driver of the car that picked us up waiting in the wings with another giddy couple. I put all of that out of my mind. We were now married!

I wanted to share the good news with mom and dad, not thinking about the time difference. After several rings, my father groggily answered. "Dad, Pat and I are in Vegas and we just got married!"

There was silence on the other end of the line. Then, in a stern, dismissive voice that told me he didn't want to talk to me, he replied, "Do you realize what time it is? I'll get your mother."

It was good to hear mom's gentle, caring voice, knowing how far she had come since the accident, but it couldn't replace the devastation of knowing that my father, whom I adored, didn't want to speak to me. Now was not the time to break the news that they were going to be grandparents again.

CHAPTER 9

COLUMBUS, NEBRASKA

It was April, and Palm Desert was becoming a ghost town. Most of the members of the club had already left for their summer homes in other parts of the country. Preparations were being made for the closing down of the club.

Pat had secured a head pro job at a brand new private club in Columbus, Nebraska before we left Lincoln. Pat's boss at the par three knew of this job opening and had recommended Pat for the job. I went with him for the interview and was hit with waves of nostalgia as we entered the small town. Columbus was about the same size as Fort Madison, with a town square and a one street downtown shopping district. It felt right.

While packing for the cross-country drive back to Nebraska, my mind was filled with many thoughts. So much had happened since my eagerly anticipated escape to a new life in California.

The thrill of the adventure and the romance of my hero

rescuing me and whisking me away to paradise hadn't panned out quite like I had anticipated. California exceeded my expectations, but coping with my hero's dark side was difficult. I wasn't sorry about my decision to stay, but I was glad we were getting away from the nightly bar scene and hoping to reestablish the closeness we shared the previous summer.

Faces of the friendly people we had met during the interview process in Columbus popped into my head, and I smiled at the prospect of getting to know them better.

Running my hand over my belly, ripples of joy ran through my body. I was going to have a baby. Due in August, it would be born in Nebraska and my dreams of marriage and family were finally coming true.

I wanted to be a mom to my child like my mom was to me. I wanted my husband to be a dad to his child like my dad was to me, providing an atmosphere of love and security. I was ready, but what about Pat? Maybe fatherhood would bring changes for the better. I worried about the drinking.

We arrived in Columbus, and were pleasantly surprised to find a spacious two-bedroom apartment waiting for us. The fourplex was made of red brick reminding me of my childhood home. It was much nicer than the apartment we had in Palm Desert. I knew in an instant we were going to be comfortable there.

Pat's immediate responsibility was to get merchandise ordered to stock the pro shop prior to opening in May. Deposits were required to open accounts with all the vendors and we had no money. Pat borrowed from the club for golf clubs, shoes, clothing, golf balls, tees, bags and all the paraphernalia necessary for the game. He would pay back the loan at the end of the season with the profits.

Members, anxious to get outdoors after a long cold, snowy winter, stopped by and introduced themselves. Pat engaged in conversation while I unpacked boxes and tagged merchandise.

Bill Curry, the owner of the club, invited us to his home for dinner. Would I ever get past my feelings of inadequacy when meeting people, especially wealthy people? My stomach churned and I had no appetite as we approached their house.

"Welcome to our home." Mrs. Curry gushed as she opened the door with stately elegance. Her friendly manner put me at ease. She was a gracious and genuine hostess. I liked her immediately.

Bill was as brash and crude as she was refined. A short stocky man with a ruddy complexion and a beer belly, he was the wealthiest man in Columbus and took pleasure in flaunting it.

"Joni, do you like the wine? It's $100 a bottle. I have it shipped by the case from Germany. You can't get it here in the states. Pat, if you need anything, anything at all just come to me. Even though we have a board it's my club you know, I own it. Hell, as a matter of fact, I own the whole damn town, so don't bother with any of those other yahoos. They all report to me, even the mayor."

After the meal, he led us down a winding staircase to his

Rathskeller. He offered Pat a cigar and began pouring after dinner drinks. Bill bragged about having built this tavern with materials brought over from Germany and hiring an architect from there to ensure its authenticity. The room was impressive with massive dark wood beams and expensive leather furniture.

The lavish bar was stocked with every kind of liquor imaginable. For the men, the night was just beginning. The glass of wine I had with dinner made me drowsy. In my pregnant state, I certainly wasn't going to have more to drink. Mrs. Curry sensed my weariness and offered a bedroom where I could lie down. I fell into a sound sleep.

When I awoke, it took me a minute or two to get my bearings. I wondered what time it might be. The blinds were drawn and I peeked through the slats to see if the sun was up. Through the early morning mist, I thought I saw something on the ground. I rubbed my eyes and looked again. There, for all the world to see, was my husband passed out on their front lawn. The embarrassment was bad enough, but I feared he would lose his job. Instead, a drinking

bond had been formed between the two men.

The Elks Country Club in Columbus, Nebraska was very

family-oriented. I knew I would be helping Pat in the pro shop, but

when they learned of my lifeguarding background, I was hired to

oversee the pool and family activities as well. The job meant extra

money for us and was a perfect fit for me. Being around the families

made me smile as I contemplated the birth of our child.

The members treated Pat like one of them and each Friday

included him in their gambling card games, while I kept an eye on the

pro shop. The card room was adjacent to the pro shop and often,

they invited me to join them, where I learned In-Between, Poker of

all kinds, Gin, and other gambling card games. Once the last

straggling golfers were in, I would close up shop and head for home,

while Pat stayed for the serious gambling and drinking.

One Saturday morning I awoke and Pat was not in the bed beside me. Knowing there would be men ready to tee it up at the crack of dawn, I dressed quickly and drove to the club. Pat was probably there, but I wanted to make sure.

I wasn't particularly worried figuring he would show up later in the day. The Club sat on a hill at the outskirts of town and it was about a thirty minute drive to our apartment. The last couple of miles were treacherous, as there were several dangerous blind curves on a dirt road. On more than one occasion, Pat had spent the night at a member's house, who lived near the club, rather than drive home in a rainstorm in the wee hours of the morning after a night of drinking and card playing.

He wasn't there and golfers were waiting in the parking lot, so I scurried around opening up the shop and getting the first foursomes out on the course. I busied myself with doing double duty in the golf shop and poolside. Lunch time came and went. *Should I call one of the wives?* I had seen Mrs. Curry from a distance at the club and she waved as if nothing was amiss. *What was I going to say? "Do you know where my husband is?"*

I closed up shop late in the evening and headed home. Sleep was impossible as my anxiety heightened and my mind whirled. Was I naïve to think he didn't come home some Friday nights because of the weather? I thought back to a night in Palm Desert when he didn't come home. A few days later, Jerry Cheney, a very flirty redhead, came up to me at the bar in Bash's. Pat had met Jerry when he first arrived in the desert and she was always trying to befriend me. I suspected they might have had more than a friend relationship by the way she came on to him. In a catty voice she said, "I hear Pat didn't come home the other night. . . wonder where he was," she added with a knowing smile.

By 6:00 Sunday morning, my frenzied state overtook my pride and I called Mrs. Curry. Frantic, I blurted out, "I am so sorry for calling so early, but Pat hasn't been home since Friday and I don't know what to do."

"He didn't tell you?" She gasped. "Oh, you poor thing. At the card game Friday night four of them decided to fly in Bill's plane to Colorado to play golf. I am so sorry no one told you. I just assumed you knew. They'll be back sometime today, they all have to be back at work Monday."

As I hung up the phone tears of relief, sadness and anger poured out of me.

Again, I dutifully opened the shop and took care of business. When Pat finally arrived home Sunday night, bleary-eyed and looking like hell from too much booze and no sleep, I confronted him.

"Didn't you care at all that I might be worried about you?"

"Yes, I should have called."

"What about the pro shop. Who did you think was going to take care of the people?"

"Joni, I said I should have called. I knew you'd be there."

141

"But how could you just go off and neglect your responsibilities?"

Hey, I'm fucking sorry. I haven't slept in days. You're overreacting. I'm here, aren't I? Everything's fine. I'm going to bed."

With that I was dismissed.

This wasn't quite like the Sunday's I recalled from childhood.

Throughout the summer, I was invited to play golf with the women and, for the most part, I enjoyed their company. Thanks to the lessons from Pat and Davey, I could hold my own. We were invited out to dinner at various members' homes. The parties they had were fun and inclusive, not stuffy and exclusive like those in the desert. Pat's ability to help people with their golf games made him their hero. A few of the wives were openly flirtatious with him. I could tell the ones who were unhappy in their marriages and probably looking for a summer fling. I tried not to be jealous, but couldn't help but think about it on the nights he didn't come home.

Pregnancy agreed with me. Other than the few days of morning sickness early on, I blossomed. I was outdoors a great deal of the time and as usual had a deep dark tan. The funky maternity bathing suits actually looked good on me. I was eating for two, so didn't worry so much about my weight and was enjoying the freedom of eating most everything I wanted.

The attention lavished on me by all the members with their comments and good wishes felt good. After a couple of baby showers the spare bedroom now had a crib and plenty of diapers and clothes for the new arrival.

The baby's due date coincided with the trial in Florida. That story he told me in the middle of the night at the Lincoln Hotel was real, and now he had to appear in court. It was a dangerous time for him and I couldn't help but worry as I dropped him off at the airport.

However, my worry was superseded by joy as mom arrived to

be with me for the birth. When I had finally gotten the courage to tell mom and dad about the baby, I was relieved when they were supportive. Mom was healthy again from all of her injuries and the two of us spent two glorious weeks together planning for the arrival of the baby. Her loving presence was medicine for my soul.

The trial ended, and Pat returned home, but no baby yet. Dad was missing mom and wanted her back home. I was sad she wouldn't be there to help when the baby arrived, but understood.

Pat had been taking flying lessons and his instructor agreed to fly mom back to Iowa, so Pat could co-pilot and get some hours towards his license. I wanted to go too, but when the pilot saw my condition and learned I was two weeks overdue he almost didn't let me on the plane. We made it over and back without incident.

Dr. Anderson scheduled a date for me to have labor induced and on September 2, 1970, I entered the hospital early in the day.

There was no panicked packing of bags and rushing to the hospital like you see in the movies. Pat dropped me off at the hospital on his way to work. I checked in and was settling into my room when Dr. Anderson came in and explained the procedure. A few minutes later he came by with a group of interns.

"Joni, would it be okay if these folks observed the birth of your baby?"

"It's okay with me." I said with a smile.

The atmosphere was warm and friendly. A nurse came in to administer the Pitocin drip to get things started. A couple of uneventful hours went by. Then, I began to feel a bit of discomfort, but nothing I couldn't handle. Suddenly, without warning, a true labor pain hit. Whoa! I had never felt pain like that . . . ever. It brought tears to my eyes. A few minutes later BAM! Another jolt. Another nurse came in and began setting up for the administration of gas. BAM! Another pain hit. The group of interns appeared at the door.

"Get those people out of here!" I shrieked.

The gas did its job and I lost consciousness. I groggily remembered being shown our beautiful baby girl before drifting off again. The night nurse came into my room around 9:00 p.m.

"Where is my husband?"

"He's out celebrating with friends." She soothed.

I started crying feeling lonely and abandoned.

The nurse rubbed my back. "You have a beautiful baby girl."

I wanted my husband rubbing my back and sharing our joy, not some nurse. Maybe having fathered other children this wasn't that big a deal for him.

For the first time in a long time I thought about God. There is no other explanation for childbirth than a miracle from God. Through tears I whispered a prayer, "Lord, thank you for blessing us with this healthy baby girl to love and cherish. I am grateful, but so sad that Pat chooses friends and drinking over being here with us. Will he ever change his ways? Please help me."

I adored being a mother and became completely absorbed in caring for little Tracy. However, instead of being there with us more, Pat took advantage of my preoccupation and stayed away more.

Tracy was an easy baby, sleeping and eating on a tolerable schedule from the beginning. The people of Columbus showered us with gifts and expressions of love. In no time at all, it was time for us to leave. Tracy was just a month old when we made the trip back to California with everyone wishing us well and anticipating our return in the spring of 1971.

When we made the trip back to Columbus, for a second summer, I was pregnant with baby number two and due in September, again. My heart was full with the anticipation of reuniting with old friends. They joked about me being in the same state of pregnancy as the year before. Much ado was made about Tracy and children of members fought over who could babysit for her. We had a one-year birthday party for her three weeks before Melissa arrived. Knowing my history of carrying my first baby past term Dr. Anderson arranged for induced labor again. The birth went smooth and a second beautiful baby girl entered our lives.

Mom came to be with me again, but this time she waited until the baby was born. Melissa was a bit cranky and colicky, and I was grateful for mom's help. However, by the time she had to go back to Iowa, the colic had subsided and I was confident I could handle things on my own.

Again, I said a small prayer of thanks for this second blessing in two short years. *How did I keep from getting pregnant all those years ago?* Maybe God had a hand in that too.

CHAPTER 10

ESCAPE TO IOWA

When Pat crossed the line from verbal to physical abuse, I became fearful. I should have left when he threatened my life and the lives of our children. I was an emotional wreck when he was around. I would do anything to avoid confrontation. If I even hinted that I was unhappy or questioned his behavior, the verbal abuses would begin.

Oh, there were moments when he lavished us with gifts and bragged about us to his friends. On Melissa's first birthday John and Mary Jo Cleland came over to help us celebrate. Pat beamed as they gushed over the girls.

"Wait, I should get the fucking video camera that we never use," Pat said, laying his smoldering cigarette in the ashtray. Several boxes wrapped in red striped paper with big red bows sat unopened on the floor. The paper was a trademark of the expensive toy store in Palm Springs. Nothing but the best for his daughter.

"I'll get the candles for the cake." I was enjoying this rare glimpse of Pat actually engaging in a family activity. He was showing off for John and Mary Jo.

John, on the floor, helping unwrap the Playskool schoolhouse, exclaimed, "These toys for kids are amazing today. They can play and learn at the same time. Pat, you went overboard with the gifts. She's only one you know."

Mary Jo and I were blowing up balloons and setting out festive paper plates with matching napkins.

"Wow John, maybe you'll make a good dad when we have kids." Mary Jo said laughing.

"Tracy, get down and help your little sister open her presents." Pat demanded. "Look at me. Smile. Wave for the camera. Joni, Joni hurry up with the fucking cake. I'll video her taking the first bite."

With the candles glow reflected in our little girl's eyes, we sang, "Happy birthday, dear Melissa, Happy Birthday to you." After ice cream and cake, Pat and John headed out the door for the local bar. *It was nice while it lasted.*

A couple of hours after he and John left, Pat called me from Bash's. A bunch of guys are here and I'm bringing them over to the house for a birthday party. Fix something for us to eat and get some extra booze, we'll be there shortly."

The click of the receiver told me this wasn't up for discussion. I scurried around straitening up the house, threw together some snacks and decided we had enough vodka, J&B and wine in the house.

The doorbell rang, and one of our golf pro friends arrived carrying a bottle of wine.

"Thanks Gary, Pat isn't here yet, but he should be any minute. Come on in."

Soon, the house was filled with people Pat had invited over. Some I knew and some were complete strangers. Chris Kristoferson was belting out *"Silver Tongued Devil and I"* on the record player someone had turned up loud. Drinks were flowing and the party was in full swing. Some asked about Pat, but most were unaware he wasn't there.

After the last guest departed, I was too tired to begin cleaning up. The mess would wait until morning. I fell asleep to the lingering smell of stale cigarettes and warm beer.

Pat arrived home in the wee hours of the morning and woke me with loud swearing and writhing in pain. He suffered from ulcers and drank Maalox like milk and took Vicodin like candy. The amount of alcohol he poured into his empty stomach aggravated the ulcers.

"Where's my Maalox," he moaned. "My goddamn gut is killing me."

He was doubled over in pain.

"Get me my fucking Vicodin."

He was a booze and pain-crazed lunatic.

Yanking open the closet door, he pulled out his shotgun. About to vomit, he stumbled into the bathroom, shut the door and locked it. I could hear the nauseating sound of puking, and I knew it wasn't all going into the toilet. He was yelling obscenities, sobbing, ranting and raving.

"Goddamnit, I can't take it anymore." He was now sobbing uncontrollably. "I may as well end it right now," he moaned.

Wide awake now, sweat began to drip down my back. I was close to panic. My voice quavered as I begged, "Unlock the door and let me in." With my face against the door, I slid down until my cheek touched the floor. "Pat, please, please unlock the door."

In his drug and alcohol induced stupor, I don't think he even heard me. Tears dripped onto the carpet, as I tried not to imagined the bloody scene if he followed through with his threat.

I couldn't call the police because of what happened the last time.

His tirade, vomiting and sobbing began to subside. I could hear heavy breathing and snoring, telling me he had fallen asleep. From far too much experience, I knew the crisis was over and he wouldn't wake until morning. There wasn't much more I could do at that point, so I climbed back into bed and tried to sleep.

I couldn't cope with what happened. When he finally emerged from the bathroom the next morning, my hysteria erupted. I pounded on his chest and screamed, "I need help. I can't think. My brain can't focus. I don't know what to do."

"Joni, what ails you? Here, just take of couple of these and you'll calm down." He held out a bottle of Valium.

"Noooo, I'm not taking any drugs."

"Yes, trust me, this'll really help you sleep, and then you'll feel better. You'll see."

"Well, maybe just a half."

He laughed a disdainful laugh and snapped, "Okay then, take a half."

That half a Valium knocked me out. I had a hard time waking up and functioned in a fog for days. I would never take Valium again.

I had to get away.

In January, I purchased plane tickets to Iowa for the girls and myself. I needed to be near people who loved me. I would tell my parents everything. I would stay in Iowa. My family would help me figure out what to do with my life.

Getting through the airport with two toddlers, luggage and a pregnant belly was exhausting. I carried Melissa and held Tracy's hand. I got stares from people that said, "Why in the world are you travelling with those children in your condition."

The attendants were helpful. The girls were excited about their first airplane ride and had books and toys to occupy themselves. While they napped I prayed we would get to our destination without serious incident.

At the gate in Moline, Illinois, the joy in my heart could not be contained as my mother wrapped her arms around me in a warm loving embrace. Dad's quick kiss on the cheek and big smile upon seeing us was medicine for my soul. He picked each of the girls up and swung then around. They loved him instantly.

My brother, David, and his family lived in Monticello, Iowa, not far from the airport, and we drove to their house to spend one night before driving on down to Fort Madison.

My sweet brother, just two years older than I, the best older brother a girl could have. Following in dad's footsteps, he was a God-fearing, wholesome family man.

"Hey Dridge," he said, with his shy smile, when he saw me. His familiar greeting, with the nickname he had given me long ago, melted my heart. He had put on a few pounds over the years, but had not lost his good looks. He was a good provider for his family, with a job as a school administrator. They had a comfortable home in this small Iowa town.

It was his daughter Lisa's seventh birthday. The occasion was festive. Everyone donned party hats. They had a younger daughter,

Misty, age four, and both girls were delighted with their two young cousins. The four of them danced around the room, laughing and singing.

David got out his movie camera, and quietly started filming the action. To the delight of my girls, when it came time for the opening of presents, Lisa was happy to let them help. The oohs, aahs and squeals of delight as each gift was revealed, a new Barbie doll or a pretty scarf, made me smile.

Later in the day, we sat around reminiscing about old times.

"Remember all the hours we spent shooting baskets in the back yard together?" David asked.

"Yah, you and dad would always risk it on the game of squares to give me a chance to win."

"How about you conning me into doing the collecting for you on your paper route, David, or selling World's Finest Chocolate for your high school fundraiser?"

Dad chimed in, "We sent you over to Harry Emerson's

confident that he would buy a candy bar. You came back crying, because he said no thank you and shut the door. I said he probably didn't recognize you and called him up and told him it was you."

"Yah, how could he say no then," David interjected.

"Then, you sent me back over and he bought the whole box." I laughed.

"Remember when we decorated our bikes together to ride in the 4th of July parade, weaving red, white and blue crepe paper in and out through the spokes and attaching a playing card to the frame with a clothespin that make a great noise when riding? Afterwards, walking our bikes back home you and your friends had firecrackers and cherry bombs that you shot off, scaring me. That was in the day before fireworks were outlawed."

"David, you were so patient, helping me with my homework at the dining room table. Remember what a huge crush my friend Cathy had on you? She always wanted to know if you were home when she came over. You flirted around with her and she loved it."

How had I ended up with a husband like Pat McCormick?

This unadulterated happiness and joy were what I had been craving. Any serious conversations could wait until we got to Grandma and Grandpa's.

Wally, my favorite cousin from childhood, happened to be visiting his parents in Fort Madison while I was there, with his wife and two daughters. A successful businessman, he was another Christian, good looking, smart man with a sweet personality. Like all the Lane men, he didn't smoke, drink or swear. When they visited the next afternoon, it was so refreshing to observe these wholesome family men interacting with my daughters.

Dad gave Melissa his watch to play with and she put it on and took it off, put it on and took it off, being like grandpa. He rocked all four girls at once in his favorite chair. They laughed and giggled as he wrestled with them on the floor.

It took the girls a while to unwind from the day's activities, and they wanted me to lay down with them at bedtime. I was going to talk to mom and dad that night, but fell asleep instead.

Dad was mayor of Fort Madison and the next day, took us to City Hall where the girls climbed on a real fire engine. He took us to his office and proudly introduced us to his staff.

Mom found joy in cooking meals for a family again and I took joy in eating her home cooking. I never could fix fried chicken the way she did, no matter how hard I tried. Helping with the dishes after the meal I thought about telling her about my circumstances, but no, I needed to tell them both at the same time.

On Sunday we went to church.

At the pre-school door a familiar voice called out, "Joni, is that you?"

"Cathleen, oh my gosh." We embraced. It was my pre-school Sunday school teacher, still at the same post after all these years.

"Are these your babies? They are adorable. And another one on the way, my oh my. Your folks tell me you are in California now."

"Yes, I am. I'm so glad to see you. I know the girls will be in good hands while we're in church."

Walking from the Sunday School building to the sanctuary, we passed so many familiar faces. Once seated in the pew, I could feel eyes on me of others realizing one of Gordon and Rosemary's children was there.

There was a calming comforting aura in that sanctuary. I could sense God's presence. I began to think about how faithful these people were in spite of their circumstances. My own parents had lost Becky, Cathleen's oldest daughter had died of an intestinal illness at the age of thirty. Mom had told me stories of other church friends who had gone through various traumas. Yet, here they were, worshiping and relying on God. Having faith in something bigger than themselves. I had to figure out a way to have their kind of faith. Sitting between my parents in that church pew, I knew I couldn't tell them my marriage was over. I couldn't bring myself to cloud their world with my ugly issues. These were my problems and I had to work them out.

A few days later as our plane descended from the sky toward the Palm Springs airport and I saw those beautiful mountain peaks again, I realized I missed those mountains, I missed the balmy winter days, I missed my friends. I had a new life now. Somehow, I had to work things out with my husband.

Pat met us at the airport. His first words were, "I didn't think you would come back."

"I didn't think I would either."

CHAPTER 11

NEW HOME OLD WAYS

After my return from Iowa, and the birth of our third child, I vowed to make my marriage work. My babies were my delight as I tolerated my husband and his behaviors. Pat had surgery for his ulcers. This alleviated the pain, and he no longer had to rely on Maalox and Valium, but there was still the alcohol.

One rare evening our whole family was home together. Becky was asleep in her crib. Tracy, Melissa and I were happily engaged in our nightly ritual of reading before bedtime. Their cute little comments and giggles, as they anticipated the turn of each page filled my heart with joy and love. Snuggled up on my bed, we had just finished "The Monster at the End of This Book" and were about to start "Pokey Little Puppy" when I heard angry shouts coming from the living room.

"You goddamn motherfucker, I put my life on the line for you, you owe me big time."

My body tensed. Who was he talking to like that on the phone?

"Every time I talk to you, you say you'll get back to me and I never hear from you. It's been over three years. I have a wife and three daughters now. I need some help here goddammit."

There was silence while Pat listened. Then his voice grew even louder.

"I don't want a fucking loan, I want payment for what I did for your precious FBI. You lying motherfucker, you made promises to me! I kept my end of the fucking deal. You got your glory and put away that fucking mafia monster and what did I get? Not a goddamned thing! That's what. You fucked me over, you hear me? I'm not hanging up the goddamn phone until you get me some money."

I got up and closed the door to the bedroom. I would never get used to the filth that poured out of my husband's mouth. It was obvious he was talking to Jim Hafley, the FBI agent from Florida.

Pat had bugged Jim for compensation ever since his bombshell testimony at the trial two and a half years ago, but hadn't had any luck. We were bursting at the seams in our small rental and needed a down payment on a house.

I finished reading, tucked the girls into their beds and kissed them goodnight.

As I walked into the living room, Pat slammed down the phone. "That really pisses me off, I'm not filling out any fucking paperwork and submitting anything. They owe me!"

"Did he offer something?" I asked.

"He wants me to apply for an SBA loan, whatever the hell that is. He said we technically don't qualify for it, but he'll try to pull some strings. It's some kind of government loan. A goddamn government loan, who the hell wants to deal with the fucking government. It could take years."

"Honey, if this will get us some money we should do it. I can help you fill out the forms. At least it's something."

Pat relented, and a couple of weeks later, we mailed the forms to Jim. It took a month or so, but Jim came through with approval at the other end.

We found a brand-new three-bedroom home under construction and paid the deposit. Pat had good taste and met often with the builder negotiating upgrades. He seemed to enjoy the process. We would visit the site together to check on the progress. Walking through the framed rooms, trying to visualize the finished product, we carried on an actual conversation.

"Watch your step, Joni, here's where the master bedroom will be."

"Wow, it looks big," I marveled.

"Now, here is the bathroom with double sinks and over here the shower."

"Where is the girl's room?"

"Oh, over here, be careful of the nails there."

"It looks nice and big, too. Maybe we could get bunk beds

with one of those cute little trundle beds underneath, so they can all sleep together."

"Yah, we can save the third bedroom for guests. Come down this way, let me show you the kitchen." Excitement filled his voice and he put his arm around me to guide me through the construction.

My heart skipped a beat. I raised my eyebrows and gave him a sideways glance. He actually put his arm around me. Did I dare hope that we might be on a path to reconstructing our relationship as we watched the construction of our home? I fantasized about the whole family sitting around the kitchen table after a home-cooked meal, laughing and talking or maybe sitting snuggled on the couch by the warm fire on a cold desert night watching TV together.

Moving day arrived. The girls rode their big wheels up and down the driveway, while I unpacked the stacks of boxes in the garage. It was a labor of love. My first real home!

I spied Pat's gun propped up in the corner of the garage. Instead of representing protection from an intruder, it was now a reminder of the night he threatened to end his life. Each time I passed by it, making trip after trip in and out of the house, another ugly memory of that night popped into my mind. That gun really bothered me. I didn't want it in this new house.

The backyard landscaping hadn't been put in yet, so the yard was bare. I found a spade and started digging a hole in the farthest back corner of the yard, next to the block wall. I labored to dig the hole deep enough so no one would ever find it. When I got it the length and depth necessary, I laid the gun gingerly down in its little grave and covered it over with the newly dug soil. I patted it down with the spade. Suddenly, with a vengeance, I stomped back and forth over the loose ground. Pat never asked about the gun.

Pat continued to obsess about money. Now, we had a hefty house payment, a loan payment and bigger utility bills. He had lived a high life in Florida and longed to live like that again.

Out of the blue one morning he announced, "Joni, I'm going to use our spare bedroom for my office."

"Your office, what do you need an office for?"

"I'm gonna start my own business. I'm gonna start booking."

"What do you mean, booking?"

"Hell, you know, taking bets. I can't make a decent living in the fucking golf business."

"Pat, you can't do this."

"Goddamn it, we need the money and I know this business."

"But, you're breaking the law. You could be arrested and taken away."

"Don't fuckin' worry, I'll be careful and besides, even if I do get arrested they won't keep me long, I've got connections."

Pat had already made up his mind and nothing I said was going to change it.

He had a separate phone line installed and began taking bets in our home. He kept the door closed to keep the kids out and the smoke-filled room from his chain smoking was suffocating.

I constantly worried about a police raid and was relieved when after a month, Pat hired Tommy Green to help with the phones and began using Tommy's apartment as his office. All of the transactions were cash, and Tommy also helped pay and collect the money. Tommy was a misfit of society. He was obese, a loner with few friends. He had a nervous high-pitched girlie laugh and creepy, blank, distant, emotionless eyes. I was always squeamish around him, and definitely didn't want him around my daughters.

Not long after Pat moved the operation to Tommy's, the police came to our house. I had gone to run errands and Mrs. Gunnemann, the wife of a retired minister, was babysitting. When I got home she calmly said, "By the way, the police were here today."

I was mortified. "Oh, I'm so sorry. Are you okay?"

"Yes, they just made the children and I sit quietly together while they searched the house."

"You must have been scared, you poor thing."

As she walked toward her car, I figured she would never babysit for us again.

I called Pat to tell him what happened, expecting him to be upset. Instead, he laughed at the thought of prim and proper Mrs. Gunnemann dealing with a police raid.

"Well, you think it's funny, but I'm scared for myself and the girls. What if they come again?"

"You dodged that fucking bullet. They won't bother with the house anymore, since they know I'm not working there."

"But, if you get arrested and put in jail, what will I do?" The thought of no income with a mortgage payment, loan payment, car payments, not to mention groceries and other daily necessities was daunting.

"Damn it, Joni, that's not going to happen, trust me."

"Can we at least hide some cash somewhere in the house just in case?"

"Will that fucking satisfy you?" he growled.

The next day he brought several thousand dollars in an envelope to the house to appease me, and we settled on a hiding place. Of course, then, I worried about someone stealing the money.

We had a checking account, but Pat only deposited enough money each month to cover the bills that couldn't be paid for with cash. There was no such thing as balancing a checkbook or a budget. If he wanted to spend he spent. I had no knowledge of our finances. The weeks he was flush with winnings, it was not unusual for him to show up with a new car, or some other extravagance. If he happened to have a losing week, he would yell at me for buying groceries.

A couple of weeks later, the inevitable raid occurred at Tommy's apartment and he called to tell me they had taken Pat to jail.

"No, Tommy!" My hand went to my throat. "I knew this would happen. Now what do I do?"

"Just stay calm," he said. "I'm on my way down to the police station now. I'll take care of it. You don't need to do anything."

Stay calm? How could I stay calm? As the hours ticked by I busied myself with cleaning, laundry and tending to the children, forcing myself to stay focused. Late in the afternoon Pat called.

"Just letting you know I'm back at Tommy's."

Relief swept through my entire body. I wasn't aware of how much tension had built up.

"Thank God, how did you get out?"

"Tommy came down and paid a fine. That's how it fucking works, Joni. Hell, all they want is a cut. Half the force bets with me. They don't really want to shut me down, they just have to keep up the façade that they care that I'm breaking the law. Gotta go, phones are ringin.'"

From then on, raids were an infrequent nuisance and I quit worrying about it.

Russ, another character among Pat's gambling cohorts, was

the complete opposite of Tommy Green. Another bookie, who worked out of Palm Springs, he and Pat became partners. He was fit, good looking and full of ego. He wore skin tight pants, silk shirts unbuttoned to reveal his hairy chest and lots of real gold jewelry. His shoes were short boots with heels and his jackets were leather. A dark-complexioned Italian he wore his brown curly hair long. He carried himself with an air that shouted, "Look at me, see how cool and handsome I am!"

Russ's girlfriend, Susie, was an attractive skinny, redhead with the kind of look older women get who do drugs and don't eat much.

Neither Russ nor Susie had children of their own, and they enjoyed the novelty of being around ours. Russ also dealt in black market movies and would bring titles such as 101 Dalmatians, The Rescuers and The Duchess and the Dirt Water Fox for the girls to watch on our VCR. One Christmas he bought them a full-sized trampoline.

The four of us often had dinner out together at one of the

finest restaurants in Palm Springs. On one occasion, when Russ and Susie arrived at our house, Susie was carrying a small plate wrapped in foil. "I brought some brownies for us," Susie announced with a wry smile.

"Have a brownie, Joni," Russ chimed in. "Susie doesn't usually bake so this is rare."

"No thanks, I don't want to ruin my appetite."

Pat grabbed a brownie off the plate and eagerly stuffed it in his mouth. This was strange as he usually didn't eat sweets, especially before dinner.

Susie laughed, "I'm having one too, Joni, come on, join us."

The three of them were giggling and playfully teasing each other like children as they ate. There was one brownie left on the plate. Susie picked up the plate and came over to where I was standing. She held it up close to my face and said, "We're all having so much fun and want you to have fun with us, here, have the last one."

Suddenly, the light went on. "Oh, I get it now, nice try, but no thanks."

"You're such a fucking prude," Pat snapped. "Forget it, you may as well just stay home."

Russ came to my defense, "Pat, don't be so harsh, Joni, come on let's go."

Pat continued to show his distain the entire evening. He either ignored me, or put me down if I attempted to participate in the conversation. As a result, I shrunk into my shell and watched in silence as they became loud, obnoxious and full of themselves under the influence of their brownies and booze.

The bookmaking business was good, really good. We joined Balboa Bay Club. Pat seldom went there, but the girls and I spent glorious days poolside.

"Tracy, do you want peanut butter and jelly on your

sandwich?"

"No, just peanut butter."

Melissa chimed in, "Peanut butter and jelly."

Becky would eat whatever I packed for her.

I peeled and cut up carrots and apples and threw in some small bags of chips as a treat. Our drinks were water and natural Hansen sodas, no sugary soft drinks.

I went through a checklist in my mind of items to take with us; cups and ice, towels for each of us, sunscreen for the girls and oil for me, diapers for Becky.

"Girls, get your cover-ups and flip flops on, let's go."

It didn't take much coaxing. They were as anxious as I was to go to the pool.

We needed to get there early to get the umbrella table by the shallow end. The pool had steps that went the width of the shallow end, so they could frolic and play in that area with me supervising from a lounge chair close by. I taught each of the girls how to swim before their first birthday, so all three of them could jump in off the side and get to the steps unassisted.

When I wanted to get in and cool off, I would take them down to the deep end where they would take turns jumping off the diving board. Tracy, almost four, and Melissa, almost three, could jump off and swim to the side without assistance, but I had to help Becky, a year and a half, with a little boost.

Skinny Tracy, in her red one-piece suit and gangly legs and arms, would start at the back of the board and run to see how far out she could jump. Melissa, in her yellow two-piece and more compact muscular little body, would walk to the end of the board, bounce a few times and then jump. Becky, with her baby belly and light blue one piece, would excitedly rush to the end of the board, stop, swing her arms back and forth, then leap to where I was in the water. It was a jaw-dropping sight for the other nervous sunbathers, drawing oohs and ahs when they saw what the girls could do.

My olive toned skin tanned easily without burning, and I

could lie in the sun for hours. This was my therapy. This was my high. The bright sunshine dancing on the water and smell of chlorine always brought back pleasant memories of the long summer hours spent at the community pool near my childhood home.

I also played tennis at the Bay Club, and took lessons from Jack Frost at Avondale Country Club. Some winter mornings it was a bit nippy when the lesson began, but it wasn't long before I shed my jacket and felt the warm rays of the sun washing over me. We were living the good life.

I wish I could say the drinking subsided, but that wasn't the case.

Pat spent very little time at home. He would leave early each morning, work into the evening and then spend the late-night hours in the bars.

In the Fall of 1974, not long after we moved into the new

house, my drunk husband stumbled into our bedroom late at night. The bedside phone went crashing to the floor, as his forehead hit the corner of the nightstand.

I leapt out of bed in horror, knowing immediately I needed help.

My fingers shook as I dialed the number of The Iron Gate, the bar where I knew Pat had been all evening. Bobby Cunard, the owner, was a friend of ours. One ring, two rings, even if Bobby was still there he might not pick up the phone at 2:00 a.m. Three rings, please, please pick up the phone, I prayed. On the forth ring Bobby answered. "Bobby, thank God you answered! Pat fell and hit his head. He's unconscious and there's blood all over. I need help, I can't lift him."

"I'll be right there."

Pat had regained consciousness by the time Bobby arrived, but was no help in his inebriated and woozy state. We managed to get him into Bobby's car. I stayed with the girls, while he drove Pat to the emergency room. The cut required several stiches and Pat had a splitting headache and nasty black eye for several days.

The incident preyed on my mind. I needed to say something, but it's hard to confront someone when they're never around.

An opportunity presented itself a few days later. Pat was seated at the kitchen table reading the paper and drinking coffee. I looked over at him from where I stood at the kitchen sink. The swelling had gone down over his eye, but it was still quite black and blue.

My pulse quickened and I knew I had to confront him. I had to be forceful and strong. I had rehearsed this over and over in my mind so many times. Looking down at the dishes I was washing, I mustered up the courage to speak. "Pat, we need to talk about the other night."

"What's to talk about, it was a freak accident. Christ, Joni, you always want to make a big fucking deal out of everything."

I had to be strong. "Well, it was a big deal for me. I was scared. I didn't know what to do. Thank God, Bobby came over. You were unconscious on the floor bleeding."

"Well he came, didn't he? Everything's fine, you fucking need to get over it."

I took a deep breath and wiping my hands with the dishtowel I walked over to where he was sitting. "You need to do something about your drinking."

"I said get over it, goddamn it, quit nagging."

Don't let him intimidate you. "I have been trying to get over your drinking since I met you. I should have left you long ago, but I didn't. At first, when it was just me, that was one thing. Then, when your verbal threats became physical, I should have left, but I didn't. We have three beautiful daughters and a new home. Instead of being a helpmate, you are a burden. I'm raising these girls by myself. Either get help or get out. I can't go on like this."

I braced myself for a torrent of profanity laced shouting. Instead, he looked up at me with a deep sadness in his eyes. Without another word, he put down the paper, grabbed his keys and walked out the door.

Wow, what just happened. I sank down in the chair he just vacated and a calm came over me. I thought I would fall apart. Yet, deep down in my heart, I knew I had to make this stand. Instead of feeling hopeless and helpless, I felt relieved and empowered. I had a glimmer of hope that I wasn't going to let myself be used and abused anymore.

Pat stayed away for several days, but when he walked back in the door he was ready to get help. He had contacted a friend of ours who had been sober for many years and Mike convinced him to seek help through Alcoholics Anonymous.

CHAPTER 12

AA/AL-ANON

I was surprised to learn that Alcoholics Anonymous had organized meetings for families of alcoholics called Al-Anon. There was a meeting room at Hope Lutheran Church just down the street from our house.

I didn't know what to expect at my first meeting, and was apprehensive. I wanted to sit unnoticed at the back of the room, but the chairs were arranged in a circle. The leader started out by introducing herself by her first name, how long she had been in Al-Anon and who the alcoholic was in her life. Each person, in turn, did the same around the circle. Some had alcoholic spouses, some parents, some children and some friends. I wasn't the only one there for the first time.

Next, the leader asked if anyone had anything they wanted to share. I sat there stunned, as people were telling my stories. Wow. My husband was a classic example of an alcoholic.

Each person was listened to with a sympathetic ear. Those who had been in the program for some time steered the conversations from focusing on the alcoholic to focusing on ourselves. I learned some new terms at that meeting. If Pat was a classic example of an alcoholic, I was a classic example of an enabler, doormat and victim. I wanted to learn how to get my husband to not drink, and here they were talking about me changing my behavior.

Al-anon taught me to get my eyes off the alcoholic and work toward improving me. I was such a Pollyanna, romantic, naïve woman and the program helped me start seeing truths about myself, and the reality of my situation. I needed to stop cowering down and catering to the alcoholic, and stop thinking of myself as poor Joni.

One aspect of the program that resonated with me, was the importance of looking to a higher power. I knew I needed God back in my life, and the AA program provided me with the impetus to reestablish my relationship with God. The powerful Serenity Prayer was recited at every meeting.

"God, grant me the serenity to accept the things I cannot change, change the things I can and wisdom to know the difference."

I read the Big Book of Alcoholics Anonymous and saw how relevant the twelve steps were to everyone, not just alcoholics. I began applying the AA and Al-Anon principles to my life.

God laid it on my heart that I needed to provide some spiritual guidance for our three girls. Pat, even though he never went to church, had insisted Tracy and Melissa be baptized as babies in the Catholic Church. Now, the girls and I began attending Palm Desert Community Church, a protestant church where I was comfortable.

For the first time since my divorce in 1965, I heard forgiveness and grace, rather than hellfire and damnation. I heard love and redemption, rather than judgment and condemnation. Could I really be worthy?

Mamie Eisenhower attended one of our church services. After the service Tracy, Melissa and little Becky were in a receiving line of children to honor her, and they each presented her with a rose. It was a touching tribute to a first lady, and I was proud that the girls got to participate.

Pat sought out the glamour and prestige of his endeavors, and it was no different with AA. He wanted to meet and hang out with the elite. We attended speaker meetings on state and regional levels. Pat learned who the AA celebrities and bigwigs were. He became friends with Bo Belinsky, a famous baseball player, and his family. They visited us at our home.

Chuck, a world-wide speaker on alcoholism and the recovering alcoholic, lived in Newport Beach a couple of hours drive from Palm Desert. Pat called him and set up a personal meeting.

Chuck was quite accommodating on the phone, and spoke of an upcoming AA convention, right there in Newport Beach. He was going to be the featured presenter at the Saturday evening speaker's meeting, open to AA members and their spouses. He suggested that he and Pat meet early Saturday morning at his home. This would free Pat up to attend the Saturday afternoon, recovering alcoholics only, meeting. He invited us to stay as a guest at his home, so we wouldn't have the expense of a hotel room. He and Pat could spend extra time together if needed.

On Saturday morning, we arrived at their beautiful spacious home, high on a hill overlooking the Pacific Ocean. Chuck was a tall, stocky older man, about sixty-five, with white hair. He welcomed us with a warm handshake and introduced us to his wife, Elsa. She was lovely, gracious and accommodating. She had obviously had a great deal of practice hosting strangers. Any fears I might have had about spending time with someone I had never met, vanished. It was a gorgeous spring day, and the men excused themselves to meet privately in a cute little gazebo area of their garden.

Elsa gave me a tour of their home and perfectly manicured grounds. She suggested we go shopping together in the afternoon, while Pat was at his meeting. I looked forward to spending more time with her. We sipped lemonade on the veranda, and visited until the men rejoined us for a light lunch on their patio. As the four of us visited and finished eating, the phone rang.

The maid called Elsa to the phone, and when she returned to the patio she announced, "I'm afraid I have some bad news. I'm in charge of our AA fundraiser, and we have a resale booth set up. The woman who was supposed to man the booth can't make it. It's too late to get anyone else, so I'm going to have to go for the afternoon. Joni, I'm so sorry, but we won't be able to go shopping."

"That's okay." I said. "I understand."

"Well, you can just come with me, although, it will be a bit boring for you," she offered.

Chuck looked over at his wife, "You know, Elsa, I'm going to the grand opening of that Vons on the other side of town." Then, turning to me he said, "Joni, why don't you come with me? My son and I are partners in a refrigeration company and our new line of freezers are being unveiled there, and I want to go check them out."

While I was contemplating which option sounded less boring, Chuck spoke with an authoritative voice. "Come on Elsa, we'll drop you at the booth, drive on over to Vons and be back in time to pick you up. Pat, we'll see you after your afternoon meeting."

The hour drive to Vons was pleasant. Portions of it were along the coastline, and I drank in the beauty of the vast expanse of water that was the Pacific Ocean.

The atmosphere at Vons was festive and crowded. Outside, row upon row of triangular little red flags fluttered in the wind. Inside, an array of colorful balloons lined every isle with free food and drink displays at every corner. We made our way to the freezer section of the store.

"There they are," he exclaimed. These freezers are state-of-the-art. They're revolutionary because they're self-contained, free standing chests that can be put anywhere in the store. Look Joni, there are no doors or lids for easy access, yet everything inside stays frozen solid. Our company is on the leading edge with this technology. Vons is putting them in all their stores."

He swelled with pride talking about this sensational product and even more proud that it was making him millions.

I had a hard time getting excited about freezers, but appreciated how he must feel. We could only look at freezers for so long, and after about thirty minutes decided to head back.

"Are you thirsty?" Chuck asked as we rode along.

"I'm okay," I said.

He swung the car into a convenience store parking lot. "Well, I'm thirsty I'll get us a couple of soft drinks."

I waited in the car.

As he maneuvered the car out of the parking space I could feel his eyes on me. "You sure have been hugging that window this whole trip, why don't you slide over here next to me?" He suggested, patting the seat.

I gave him a sideways glance, not only because of what he had just said, but also because of the lecherous tone in his voice.

"No, I'm fine," I managed as I gripped the door handle tight.

"Open the glove box," he commanded.

I opened the glove box.

"Take that magazine out."

As I removed it from the glove box, I could tell it was a pornographic magazine. I was expecting to see pictures of scantily clad women on the cover, but instead, there were pictures of men in various provocative poses.

He reached out as if to take the magazine, but instead, pulled back the cover as if trying to help me open it.

"Turn to the centerfold." The centerfold could be unfolded twice, making it three full pages wide. "Open up the whole thing," he said impatiently.

There between us was a full-length layout of Jim Brown, the black football player. He was lying on his back, propped up on one elbow with his body turned fully toward us. He was completely nude and his gigantic, erect penis was smack dab in the middle of the centerfold. I sat perfectly still, averting my eyes from the page.

The tone of Chuck's voice changed from lecherous to melancholy and he began to ramble. "You wouldn't know the ravages of alcohol and what it can do to a man's body." He stared straight ahead as if in a trance. "I'd give anything to have a penis like that. I haven't been able to get it up since I was a much younger man because of alcohol. I haven't had a drink for many years, but the damage was done long ago. It's too late and I'm too old." He was lost in memory about what he had lost.

Suddenly, just when I thought he forgot I was there, he brought me back into the picture. "You know, Joni, I travel all over the country speaking about alcoholism and I get lonely. Why don't you come along and be my travelling companion? You wouldn't have to do anything, just be there with me." He had a dreamy look on his face. "I'd be happy with a young, beautiful woman by my side. People would think I was a lucky, potent, virile guy." He paused for a minute, and I knew he looked over at me. I didn't dare look back.

"Wouldn't that be nice? You'd get to see many parts of the country, maybe even go overseas. I know all about what it's like being married to an alcoholic and dealing with all their struggles. I'll take you away from all of that."

The remainder of the drive, he continued to ramble and fantasize until we neared the building where his wife was waiting. I quietly folded up the magazine, and put it back into the glove box. He parked the car, and, in silence, we got out and walked inside the building.

Elsa gave us a cheery greeting. "There you are. How was your afternoon?" Not waiting for an answer, she babbled on. "Joni, you made the right choice. Not many people came by and the afternoon dragged. We'd have had a much better time shopping."

Chuck and Elsa exchanged small talk in the front seat on the short drive back to the house, with her doing most of the talking. When we got there, Elsa offered me some refreshment.

"I think I'll lie down before dinner if you don't mind." I

answered.

I went to our guest room and lay down on the bed. My mind was awhirl. I couldn't ignore what happened. I thought of alcoholic women who went to this man for help. How much more would he screw up someone who was already screwed up? What will his wife say or do if I tell her? How do I tell her? Will she believe me? What should I do? I'll tell Pat first and see what he says.

About thirty minutes later, Pat returned from his meeting. I told him what happened. He agreed I had to tell Elsa, but should wait until after the evening's festivities.

Chuck and Elsa were the guests of honor, and sat at a special table during dinner, so I was spared having to chit chat with them. Chuck was introduced as the speaker, to a standing ovation. My stomach churned. I tried to focus on the content of what he was saying, but had lost all respect for the man. At the end of his talk, the crowd again stood, clapping with admiration. He was their hero.

Back at the house, Pat and I went into the living room and sat down on the sofa. Elsa came in announcing that Chuck was tired and had gone straight to bed. This was my chance to speak. My palms were sweaty and my heart was pounding in my chest. Pat spoke first.

"Mrs. Chamberlain, could you sit down with us for a minute? Joni has something we think you ought to know."

He looked over at me and nodded.

My throat was dry. Slowly, I began to tell her what had happened that afternoon. Elsa listened without much expression until I finished.

I could feel sweat between my legs. *Please say something I begged.*

When she spoke, her voice was very soft and sad. "Joni, you are so brave for telling me this, it had to be so hard to do. I am so sorry you had to experience it. I feel partly responsible, because I let him take you with him. I have been in denial about his behavior. I had a similar report recently, but not quite as graphic as yours. It concerned me, but I dismissed it as an isolated incident. Now, with what you are telling me, I know I need to confront the problem." She lowered her head and began to weep. "He won't be able to travel and speak, because there are too many opportunities for things like this to occur. Thank you so much for having the courage to tell me."

I cried tears of relief, releasing all of the tension that had built up in me, but I also cried tears of sadness, that someone as revered as Chuck, would no longer be allowed to help those in need.

As the weeks went by, I often thought about that encounter, but was able to keep my faith in the AA program and continue attending Al-Anon meetings. I could feel myself getting stronger as a person, and not allowing Pat to intimidate me as much. However, the danger of him returning to booze was now a veiled threat, another way of controlling me.

Through my exposure to AA, I learned of a startling phenomenon among alcoholics called "dry drunks." The alcoholic may not be drinking, but still exhibit behaviors very similar to when they were drinking. Unless the alcoholic was willing to follow the twelve steps, as outlined in the big book of Alcoholics Anonymous, and uncover the cause of the drinking, the odds of drinking again were high.

A few months into his sobriety, one rare afternoon when Pat was home he erupted into one of his demeaning filthy mouthed temper tantrums over something inconsequential in front of the children, I snapped. "I am so sick and tired of listening to your selfish, self-serving rants and demands. You have no respect for me and no concern for these children. All you care about is yourself. But I guess you don't really care about yourself either do you, or you would be doing something to change. I used to love you, but I don't anymore. I hate you. I hate you, I hate you. Come on girls, we're leaving."

I hustled the three girls into the car and drove away with no plan or destination in mind. We had met a couple at one of the regional meetings of AA and the wife and I hit it off. They lived in San Juan Capistrano. We exchanged phone numbers and addresses and she said to call if I ever needed anything. I didn't call, I just showed up at their door. We had nothing but the clothes on our backs.

This couple must have been in a state of shock, but these generous people bedded us down that night under blankets, on their living room floor. Staring up at the ceiling, I imagined bugs crawling over me, and longed for the comfort of my king-sized bed. What was I thinking? I wasn't thinking. *I don't even know these people.* I didn't realize they had three teenage boys. They can barely make ends meet, let alone take care of us. I waited for the first light of dawn, and before anyone else got up, I gathered the girls and drove back home.

I walked in the door and was greeted by an icy stare. *Maybe this wasn't going to be as easy as I thought.*

"What are you doing back here?" He growled.

"This is our house. This is where we belong."

"Oh no you don't. You can't walk out on me like you did, and then think you can just fucking walk back in, as if nothing happened."

What about all those times you walked out as if nothing happened.

I walked over to where he was sitting, and sat down at his feet. I had to convince him I was sorry. "I was angry," I managed to say, looking up at him. "I'm sorry, I lost my temper." I didn't mean what I was saying and he knew it.

"You said you hate me," he said, in an accusing tone.

I moved to the arm of his chair, put my hand on the back of his neck, drew his lips to mine, kissed him and said, "I didn't mean what I said. I don't want to leave. Please forgive me."

I realized I needed to have a plan. I needed a job. I needed time to get my act together before I could begin to think about being

200

on my own.

CHAPTER 13

NEW FAMILY

In the spring of 1974, Pat hired Lawrence Talbot, a private investigator, to help locate his birth mother. I was curious, yet, apprehensive. If he found this woman then what? Would he hate her for giving him up? What if she didn't want to see him? Would he suffer more psychological damage to his already damaged psyche? Maybe it could help him sort some things out in his life. How would this affect us? He couldn't show love and affection for those of us he already had, how was he going to deal with someone he never knew? It seemed like a huge gamble and certain to be a source of added emotional turmoil, but I wasn't going to stand in his way. If it was important to him, he needed to do it.

Six months later, on a cool October night I was in the bathroom toweling off the girls as they chattered and giggled fresh from bath time. I heard the phone ring and then Pat's voice. The words were muffled through the closed bathroom door, but his serious tone and polite manner of speaking told me this wasn't one of his cronies.

I hurriedly dressed the girls in their fresh jammies and sent them to their room, telling them I would be in shortly to tuck them in and read them a story. As I tidied up the bath room and made trips to the laundry room with wet towels and dirty clothes, I paused in the hallway hoping to catch bits and pieces of his conversation. "Is this an older brother?" He asked.

There was a pause as Pat listened.

"Does she have any other brothers or sisters?"

When I was within earshot again, I heard, "What kind of heart condition?"

Oh my gosh, this must be about his mother!

"Okay, well thanks for the information, yeah, go ahead and give him my phone number. I'll be in touch."

I read one short story to the girls, anxious to hear about the conversation.

I tiptoed into the dark living room. I could see the red glow of his cigarette brighten, as he sucked the smoke into his mouth. After a couple of seconds pause, he inhaled deep into his lungs. He held his breath, before releasing a long exhale.

I stood near him, my hands clasped together near my heart. "Was that about your mother?"

He took another long drag on the cigarette, digesting what he had just heard. "Yeah, that was Talbot. He located my mother's older brother George who still lives in Montana. George told Talbot his little sister, Sue, got knocked up by that wild and crazy son of the Carolyn family, one of the biggest cattle rancher's in the valley. They called him "Lucky." His reputation as a drinking, gambling womanizer was well known. He had no intention of marrying her. Their mother refused to acknowledge Sue's condition. George said he was the only person she had to help her. Knowing there was no way she could keep the baby, when her time came, George drove her to the hospital and helped make adoption arrangements with the doctor."

I slowly lowered myself down onto the edge of the sofa. I wanted to reach out and touch him, to hold him close, as he processed this news about the woman who gave him life. But I knew better than to try, by the way he shrank back when I sat next to him.

"George said his only hesitation about contacting her now was concern about a mild heart condition she had, and the affect this news might have on her health. My mother lives in Arlington, Virginia with her husband, Carter Quinlin, a retired Air Force guy. They have one married son, Mike. Neither of these men knows anything about the fact that she gave birth to a baby out of wedlock, all those years ago."

Other than a couple more drags on his cigarette, Pat showed little emotion as he talked. He just stared straight ahead, stone faced.

"Talbot said George agreed to take my phone number and would call me in a few days after he had time to mull all this over."

Pat leaned his head back on the couch and closed his eyes.

Again, I wanted to wrap my arms around him and hold him close, but I sat quietly with my hands in my lap. The door was open. No more wondering or fantasizing about this woman. We now had real information, with real human beings involved.

George called a couple of nights later, and the two of them talked for quite some time. They agreed that George would call Sue and tell her what had transpired. That way, she could decide what she wanted to do without feeling pressured.

George called again the very next night. He explained that Sue had been silent on the other end of the phone when he broke the news. When she spoke, she said she had never given up hope of one day receiving such a call. As a military couple, she and her husband traveled far and often. Each time they were in a new area, she would go through the phone book on the off chance she would find his name. George gave her our number.

Sue contacted Pat discreetly by phone the very next day. Within a week, after a couple of lengthy phone conversations, Pat agreed to fly to Virginia for a clandestine meeting. If they both were content with simply meeting each other, then, going their separate ways, she would have no reason to reveal any of this to her family. They met for dinner at the hotel where Pat was staying. He flew home the next day.

I was so anxious about this meeting, I could hardly focus on laundry, meals and tending to the needs of the girls. I kept looking at the clock and calculating the time difference. Was it three hours? Three hours earlier or three hours later? Were they meeting right now? What were they saying? Did they touch or hug? Probably not. I tossed and turned all night, envisioning this emotional encounter. I worried Pat wouldn't reveal to her how important this was to him.

When he walked in the door I wanted to know everything.

"How did it go?"

"I'm not sure."

"Did you like her?"

"Yes, she seems like a really nice lady."

"Are you going to see her again?"

"I don't know, she was kinda hard to read."

"Do you want to see her again?"

"Yes, but not if she isn't interested."

When I pressed for more detail he snapped, "That's all there is to tell damn it."

The next week, Pat received a small formal monogrammed note card from his mother. He brought it over to where I was sitting. With a dejected tone in his voice he read it aloud.

"Pat, it was wonderful getting to see you as a grown-up man. You are so handsome. I have thought about you a thousand times and wondered what it would be like to know you. Thank you so much for making the trip to Virginia and meeting with me. I wish you all the best and understand if you don't want to pursue the relationship any further. Thank you again for a wonderful evening. Sue"

Pat's face fell as he read the words. "Well, that's it I guess."

"Are you kidding me?!" I jumped up off the sofa, turned to face him and blurted out, "You are both so afraid to show your emotions. She just met the baby she gave away nearly forty years ago and that's it? Pat, I don't believe you went to all this trouble to find her just to let it die. She thinks you don't want to pursue the relationship. Look me in the eye and tell me how you feel about the meeting and what you really want."

His eyes filled with tears and with a quaver in his voice he managed to say, "I want to have her in my life."

"Then you need to let her know that. Call her, let her know you got her note and honestly tell her how you feel."

They ended up conversing by phone several more times and agreed they wanted to pursue the relationship.

Sue told her husband and son the whole story.

After that hesitant first step, changes began to happen

rapidly. In March of 1975, she and her husband moved to San Juan Capistrano. We visited them there, where the girls and I met her for the first time, and we all met her husband for the first time.

Sue Quinlin was a tall, small-boned woman who carried herself with dignity. She was intelligent and well spoken. Her years as the wife of a military officer groomed her in the social graces. I liked her immediately.

There was an underlying iciness between her and her husband, that wasn't the result of these recent developments. He referred to her as Susie Q, and with distain in her eyes she shot back, "You know I don't like it when you call me that."

Carter, her husband, was stout, smoked cigars and threw his weight around like you would expect from a military senior officer used to being waited on. He tolerated us and she tolerated him.

Four months later, they bought a house in Palm Desert, just a few streets away from us. Being a strong-willed woman, once Sue made up her mind to have this long-lost son in her life, nothing would stop her. She became Grandma and he became Carter to the girls.

A short time later, their son, Mike, and his wife, Silvia, moved from Georgia to a house twenty minutes away from us in Palm Springs. They had an adopted son Sean, just a year older than our oldest daughter, Tracy. They obviously had no strong ties to where they had been living.

Mike was not very tall and slight built like his mother. He was reserved and quiet. I sensed he was a disappointment to Carter, his father. Mike's wife was a heavy-set bossy woman. The two of them had an underlying dislike of each other.

It was clear from the start that the stepbrothers had very little in common. Pat offered Mike a job helping in his bookie business, but Mike would have nothing to do with something illegal, and ended up working for the government as a mail carrier. Mike didn't smoke or drink, so wouldn't go out to the bars at night, and after a couple of failed attempts to include Mike in his life, Pat quit trying.

It was an interesting dynamic of three dysfunctional groups of people, all putting up a façade, in an attempt to construct a functional family.

CHAPTER 14

RELAPSE

It was April of 1975 and having spent the last two summers in the desert I knew about those 110-degree days when the car door handle burnt my fingers, the pool decking burnt my bare feet and it felt like a furnace blast hit me when I walked outside. I wanted a pool in our yard.

When I mentioned it, Pat's initial reaction was, "Joni, you don't need a fucking pool. You can swim at the neighbors and you have the Bay Club."

"I know, but I can only go to the neighbors when she invites me, and I feel like we're imposing. I think she is uneasy when I am there with three children under five years of age. We can't just go there and swim by ourselves, she feels like she has to be out there supervising, she's old and worries."

"Where the hell would we put a pool, our back yard is too narrow."

"What about the side yard?"

"It would be completely hidden from the house."

"What if we put a big window in along that side?"

"Are you fucking kidding me! We're not knocking a hole in the wall of our new house."

Surprised by my persistence, I kept talking.

"If we had a pool I would swim laps every day. It would be great exercise. Can't we just have someone tell us if it would be feasible or not?"

"Hell, I guess I could have Fred come over and take a look, but don't get your hopes up."

I couldn't believe my ears. He was considering it.

The details were worked out, and by summer I had my window and my pool.

It was a year of adjustment. Sobriety had its ups and downs, but I was beginning to think maybe we were making positive progress. Pat had just received his AA chip for one year of sobriety.

It was my 30th birthday. The twenty-minute drive from Palm Desert to Palm Springs was pleasant. Pat and I chatted comfortably enjoying a night out together, just the two of us.

Always a great storyteller, he related a funny bar incident from when he used to go to Palm Springs before we met. I spontaneously laughed out loud at the punch line with no inhibition. What a glorious feeling of freedom to be myself. Pat had suggested Banducci's because it was one of the first places we stopped when we arrived in Palm Springs in 1969, just six years earlier. It was a sweet gesture indicative, of his changed behavior without alcohol.

We settled in to a romantic booth and my mind turned to thoughts of the first time I was there. The bartender had come running out from behind the bar when he saw Pat and the two of them embraced like long lost brothers. Pat introduced me proudly and we sat down at the bar and ordered a drink. Giddy with excitement of finally arriving in Palm Springs, I was oblivious as to how quickly the two men forgot I was there. We never did eat there that night, but went there often over the years for the great Italian food.

As I reminisced, I heard the waitress ask, "What can I get you to drink?"

"Two glasses of Chianti," Pat blurted out without hesitation.

Abruptly I was brought back to the present. My eyes widened and my stomach tightened,

"What are you doing?" I gasped.

"Joni, a little wine won't hurt anything. I can have one glass. Besides, it's your birthday."

He may as well have punched me hard in the stomach. Immediately my guard went up. I was scared. I watched him intently like I used to in the bars in Lincoln, Nebraska, but it was different this time because I had a knowledge I didn't have before. I recognized the way he savored the alcohol in his mouth. The way his body relaxed more with each swallow. Suddenly, every dark and evil drunken nightmare from the past flashed before my eyes.

"Come on, lighten up. Let's have a little fun. I'll order you your favorite, Cannelloni."

The booze took over. He continued to talk incessantly, no longer to me, but through me.

Fear washed over me like a giant wave. I was nauseous, my appetite gone. I disappeared from his view.

The escalation from one glass of wine to out of control was rapid, and Pat soon returned to his old ways. One month later, he went on an Alaskan fishing trip with Tommy Green and a couple of other cohorts. I was beyond questioning any of his plans and didn't care if they didn't include me. The scars of abuse were etched deep.

He was going to be gone for about ten days and I was looking forward to it. The girls and I could enjoy our home, and I could sleep soundly with no middle of the night interruptions. We spent carefree laughter filled days in and out of our new pool. We had friends over. We stayed in our bathing suits until it was time for pajamas at night. The tension drained from my body.

The ten days flew by. The morning he was to return, old feelings of apprehension and tension began stirring and building in me. I wondered what time he might actually show up, or if his plans had changed, which they often did. Late in the afternoon, as the really hot part of the day was easing just a bit, I heard a car pull up out front.

The girls and I were poolside as usual. The side gate by the far end of the pool swung open and there stood Pat. I should say, there swayed Pat. He stumbled toward the pool in a drunken stupor.

He began taking off his shoes and socks, steadying himself with the diving board. He stripped to his briefs and, feet first, slid into the water. Taking a gulp of air, he disappeared beneath the surface. I could see his distorted form underwater as he neared the shallow end where I was sitting. He reappeared near the edge, by my feet, water dripping from his red, puffy face and bloodshot eyes. He began to vomit. It wasn't a violent upheaval, just three or four slow motion, roiling upchucks. The retching and undulation of the water seemed to be happening in rhythm. His head was just above the edge of the pool, causing some of the putrid bile to dribble into the water and some to spew onto the deck and trickle toward me, forming a slimy puddle under my lounge chair.

The hot, dry desert air that I loved, became tainted with a fermented sickly sour stench. I hated him. I wished he were dead. I had never hated anyone or wished anyone dead in my life, and these thoughts terrorized me.

Somehow, he made his way out of the pool and into the house. The girls were still frolicking in the water, oblivious to what had just transpired and I sat there, immobilized. The foul smell under my chair brought me to my senses. I had to clean off the deck and prepare something for dinner. For the next couple of hours, I busied myself with the tasks at hand. I found Pat, naked, sprawled across our king-sized bed, snoring with that ugly snorting sound of a passed out drunk, that I knew all too well. I closed the bedroom door and went about the routine of settling the girls down for the night. The air had gone out of our ten-day bubble. We were all a little quieter that night, not as much laughter, not as much freedom to be us. I knew they could feel it, too.

I couldn't go back into our bedroom that night. I pulled extra bedding from the hall closet, and tucked the sheets into the cushions of the couch. I opened up the slider to the back yard, and was grateful for a cool gentle breeze that wafted in. Moonlight bathed the patio, and I sat down outside for a while, digesting my thoughts. As I gazed up at the stars in the night sky, I could feel God looking back and saying, "This is not how life is supposed to be."

Once again, I had to make a stand.

The following morning, the girls and I had already had our breakfast and I was cleaning up the kitchen, when Pat stumbled in and plopped down at the table. He was a disheveled mess. His eyes were bleary and bloodshot, he was unshaven, still reeking of alcohol and vomit, a lovely sight. His head had to be pounding, but I didn't care.

Full of anger, with clenched fists, I stormed over to where he was sitting. "Pat, I'm done."

"Listen, Joni, please. I feel like hell, not now."

"No, you listen. Alcohol has such a hold on you and you can't admit it. If the AA program hasn't convinced you of this, there is nothing I can do. If you can't see it, I can't see it for you." Full of hate and loathing, I reminded him of what he was losing. "You have a beautiful wife and three beautiful daughters. We are full of life, positive energy and love. Your presence brings ugliness, negativity and a scary darkness. It is too big of a burden for me to bear. You need to leave."

221

He stood up from the table and shuffled slowly down the hall to the bedroom.

Even knowing I was doing the right thing, it took everything within me to let him go. The teachings of the AA program told me I couldn't save him, but my natural urge to mother and nurture welled up inside. Fear gremlins in my head fought for attention. How will the children and I manage? I don't want to be alone. Will he retaliate? What about our friends? What will dad say?

He grabbed his still packed toiletry bag from the night before, along with one of the suitcases full of clothes and left. I didn't know where he was going and I didn't care.

CHAPTER 15

JOB

This time I was more rational. I began to scour the help wanted section of The Desert Sun newspaper. With my golf background I was confident I could find a job at one of the many clubs in the desert. I may have to settle for a receptionist job, but it would be a start. The trouble was, by October most of the positions were probably already filled. I wanted to find something in Palm Desert, so I wouldn't have too far to drive. After a week or so, a small ad caught my eye.

"Eisenhower Medical Center – Collector's Corner looking for Office Manager."

I certainly knew about Eisenhower Medical Center, but what was Collector's Corner? Office Manager might be more than I'm qualified for, but it would probably pay better.

The ad said to apply at the Personnel Office of the Medical Center, so the next day I went there. The bulletin board was covered with open positions for doctors, nurses and administrators. I felt out of place. When I told the receptionist I was there to apply for the Office Manager job at Collector's Corner, she led me into a large room open room. There were several people busy at typewriters, some sitting at tables writing and still others engaged in personal interviews. My hands were sweaty and my mouth was dry. I could feel my heart beating inside my chest. I kept telling myself to stay calm. I was put through a battery of clerical tests. The following day, I received a call advising me to report to Collector's Corner in Rancho Mirage for a personal interview.

Mary Anger, the volunteer in charge of Collector's Corner, and two other volunteers, Hazel Jaggar and Doris Marks conducted the interview. The three of them were delightful. I was struck by their poise, warmth and genuineness. Rather than feeling intimidated, I felt comfort in their presence.

During the interview, they filled me in on the history of Eisenhower Medical Center and Collector's Corner. In 1966 Bob and Dolores Hope donated 80 acres of land for a new hospital to serve the rapidly growing Coachella Valley. Funds from the Palm Springs Desert Classic golf tournament, renamed the Bob Hope Desert Classic in 1965, helped finance the construction. General and Mrs. Dwight D. Eisenhower consented to naming the hospital for the former President.

Dolores Hope was named President of the Board of Trustees and in 1969 Bob Hope emceed groundbreaking for Eisenhower Medical Center. Dolores also spearheaded the formation of the Eisenhower Medical Center Auxiliary.

They renamed the main street in front of the site Bob Hope Drive and in 1971 the Medical Center admitted its first patient. In 1972, then Vice President Spiro T. Agnew dedicated one of the new Professional Buildings under construction. Millions of dollars were raised and donated by various prominent desert residents through fundraising functions from private parties to gala events.

There was a dedication ceremony for Collector's Corner, this

5,000 square foot resale store for the purpose of raising funds for Eisenhower Medical Center.

In late 1975, when I began my quest to find a job, Eisenhower Medical Center was a prime source of employment. Donating to Eisenhower Medical Center was the thing to do for the rich and famous, and it seemed like every week a new building or wing of the hospital was being dedicated.

The plan was to staff Collector's Corner with volunteers from the Hospital Auxiliary, but they needed one paid employee to coordinate over fifty volunteers, make bank deposits, operate the cash register, hire a driver for the delivery truck and perform general office duties.

It could have been my brief experience at La Quinta Country Club that caught someone's eye, because many of the volunteers were members there, but for whatever reason they liked me, and I was hired.

The main floor of Collector's Corner was one big room

where the donated merchandise was displayed. I had a clear view of the main room from my work area behind a long two tiered counter, and could assist on the floor if necessary. My typewriter and workspace were on the lower level of the counter. The upper level was used for the merchandise brought up to be purchased. Mary Anger and I were the only ones allowed to ring up sales on the large cash register at the center of the counter. The receiving room was at the back of the building with floor to ceiling roll-up doors, and trucks could easily back right up to those doors to load or unload. There were various sized tables, clothing racks and plenty of storage space available for items to be received, tagged and priced before being taken out onto the main floor for sale.

I had never met a woman like Mary Anger. I was mesmerized by her strength and confidence. She was in complete control of the store, especially the pricing of donated items. She came in almost every day, but if a shipment came in when she wasn't there, and someone else priced a high-ticket item and put it out on the floor, she could live up to her name of Mary Anger in an instant.

Mary entered the store one morning and came up to where I was sitting behind the counter.

"Good Morning, Joni. How are you?"

"I'm fine Mary, how are you?"

"Oh, I didn't sleep very well last night, my arthritis was acting up. But that happens a lot, just part of getting old."

She was probably in her seventies, but had the energy of someone much younger. She dressed elegantly and always wore lots of gold jewelry. Her thin-stacked bracelets made a clinking noise when she raised or lowered her arms, and she had rings on almost every finger.

I glanced up and saw that her eyes did look a bit tired.

"Sorry to hear that, do you want some coffee?"

"No thanks, I had enough at home."

She donned her volunteer smock, emblazoned with the red, white and blue Eisenhower Medical Center logo, and strolled leisurely out into the floor to peruse the merchandise.

I returned my attention to my paperwork. About ten minutes later I heard her quickened footsteps approaching the desk. It wasn't a good sound.

"Who priced this lamp and put it out on the floor?" She snapped.

I looked up, and her once tired eyes were now ablaze with fury. Her long, manicured nails were tapping nervously on the countertop. She was holding a small table lamp with a shade.

"I don't know." I managed to say.

"Well, I need to find out. It's a good thing I found this before someone got out of here with a steal." She turned abruptly and headed for the receiving room ready to pounce. I could hear her from where I sat. "Judy, did you put this lamp out?"

"Yes, I did," Judy replied.

"You don't know anything about the value of this lamp. This price is ridiculously low. When it comes to this type of merchandise, you are to set it aside until I have a chance to see it. Do you understand? We're here to make money for the hospital, not give things away. Did you price and put any other items out on the floor?"

"Yes, I'm sorry, Mary."

"Well then, let's find them and see what else you've done before it's too late."

The volunteers that worked at Collector's Corner either acquiesced to her demanding ways, or went to work elsewhere in the volunteer organization.

Mary had her favorite buyers. She knew what kinds of things they were looking for, and would call them and have them come look before an item was even put on display. She had a keen sense of value, and knew what prices would be tempting to the buyer, but still get top dollar for the hospital.

One of her favorite shoppers, Bob Cunard, the man who came to my rescue when Pat fell and hit his head, owned The Iron

Gate restaurant in Palm Desert.   He also had a big home and restaurant in La Quinta. When a unique piece was donated, she called him.

"Hello Bob, its Mary. An exquisite, antique, hand carved side table just came in I think you could use. You need to come today and look at it, because I need to get it out on the showroom floor."

Within an hour or two, Bob arrived and the dance began.

"Wow, it's beautiful, but I think it's too big for the space I'm trying to fill."

"Are you sure?"

"What do you want for it?"

"$4,500."

"Are you crazy? I can get a new one for close to that."

"Yes, but this is an antique. You know you don't want a new one.   Look at the detail." She sashayed slowly around the piece, pointing out the hand carvings and marble drawer pulls.

"It's probably too big."

"Let's measure it."

"Hmmm. Well, it would probably fit. It is gorgeous. I'll give you $4,000 for it."

"Bob, you know it's worth way more than that."

"Yeah, but $4,000 is all I'll pay."

"Okay then, I'll put it out on the floor at $4800 and see what happens."

"How about $4200?"

"Sold."

She was a master at making a deal, and beamed with delight when she got her price. I watched in awe as she worked her magic time and time again. The other volunteers put in their time, but she worked it like it was her own business. I needed to be more like her.

I was so grateful for my job. It was real. It was all mine and it gave me a sense of worth and accomplishment. I had pursued and secured the job as a means of escaping my marriage, but it was giving me so much more. A sense of financial security and the boost to my self-esteem were what I needed, but the added perk of getting the inside scoop on the rich and famous was pure fun.

When Frank Sinatra married his new wife Barbara, she wanted to get rid of the old furniture and redo the house to her taste. There was nothing wrong with what they had, she just wanted to make it her own. Many of the volunteers were personal friends of the Sinatra's, and shared first hand titbits of gossip about the couple as they sat pricing and tagging the truckload of merchandise from their home.

The Auxiliary had put together a cookbook entitled "Five Star Favorites – Friends of Mamie and Ike." One day Dolores Hope and Alice Faye spent the day at Collector's Corner autographing cookbooks.

I could feel myself becoming stronger as a person every day. I had always been a good mother and continued to relish that role. I was bolstered by the Al-Anon support that focused on me being the best me I could be. My job was a gift from heaven.

I hadn't heard from Pat for a few weeks, but eventually the phone call came. After the initial small talk, he said, "I'm going to AA meetings again."

"Good for you." I was polite, but noncommittal.

"I got my three-week chip at the meeting the other night."

"That's a step in the right direction."

"I want to move back home."

I wasn't expecting that. I didn't want him there.

"No, I think it's too soon."

"But that is our home, you are my family, and I should be there."

He knew what words to use to tug at my heart strings. He was trying again. Could he really change? He's my husband. If he's willing to try, I need to acknowledge that and try, too.

"Okay, but I'm not promising anything."

I began attending Al-Anon meetings again, knowing I needed help in sorting things out for myself.

CHAPTER 16

CHANGE OF PLANS

Any physical attraction I had for my husband had died long ago. I viewed him as someone who needed help, more of a mother/child relationship than husband/wife. I avoided going to bed at the same time he did, either feigning sleep or falling asleep before he came in or, if he went first, hoping he would fall asleep before I came in. I slept with my back turned and as close to my side of the bed as possible. Any attempts at intimacy on Pat's part made me cringe.

As hard as I tried to avoid having sex with my husband, there were times when it wasn't possible, if I were to keep up the charade. When he used to come home drunk, he would just force himself on me to satisfy his need. Sober, he didn't demand sex in a drunken stupor any more, but wanted me to be in the mood along with him. I couldn't make excuses all the time without arousing suspicion.

Having birthed three children, I knew what morning sickness

felt like. I tried to ignore it. I would lay awake at night trying to will the feeling to go away. I prayed for this not to be true. I thought I was being careful. I stewed about it until I couldn't stand it any longer.

I stared at the doctor in disbelief when he handed me the news, even though I knew the answer. I cried. He thought they were tears of joy.

What would Pat say? How could I start all over with a new baby? With Becky starting kindergarten next year, there was finally a light at the end of the tunnel. Was it a boy or girl? With my other pregnancies, I had hoped for a boy. I loved Tracy, Melissa and Becky with all my heart, but if I had to be pregnant, the only thing that might save my sanity would be for this little life to be male. What about my plan to become independent and escape my abusive marriage? Would I have to give up my job? How would the girls react to having a new baby in the house? They would probably be thrilled.

Pregnancy always agreed with me, and this time was no different. The thought of another little life growing inside of me brought on that euphoric feeling of nurturing and motherhood. As the months went by, I radiated in my pregnancy. The girls were as excited as little six, five and three-year-olds could be, not really knowing what to expect. Pat bragged to his cronies that we were having another child. I craved green beans and would stand at the kitchen sink eating them straight out of the pan.

When it came time to wear maternity clothes, Russ and Susie bought me several very expensive outfits from an exclusive maternity store in Palm Springs. My friends had a baby shower for me.

True to my pattern, the baby was overdue. I was scheduled for induced labor on May 24, 1977. Pat and I arrived at Desert Hospital in Palm Springs early on delivery day. Once I was settled in the room, we were told it would be a few hours before anything started happening, so, Pat left saying he would be back in plenty of time. After a few hours of the Pitocin drip, the subtle pangs of the beginning of labor began, and the doctor came in to evaluate my status.

"Does your husband want to be in the delivery room?" He asked.

"I don't know, can he?" No doctor had ever posed that question to me before.

"Sure, we didn't used to encourage it, but now it's pretty common."

"Well, it's okay with me, I would like that."

When Pat returned, I told him what the doctor had proposed.

"No fucking way. I couldn't handle it."

The doctor came in just before they wheeled me into the delivery room, looked over at Pat and said, "Here put these on," and threw him a set of scrubs.

Already groggy from the gas, I thought I saw Pat enter the

room, then I was out.

From far away I heard voices. Where was I? Slowly the realization hit that I was in the hospital. *Did I have the baby yet?* I opened my eyes, and the nurse looked down at me and said, "Oh, there you are. Are you ready to see your new baby?"

"Yes."

I wanted to ask if it was a boy, but I was afraid of the answer.

Pat leaned over the bed, kissed my forehead and placed this precious little bundle on my stomach and softly announced, "We have our boy."

To say that tears of joy ran down my face would be a gross understatement. My entire body breathed a staggering sign of relief. Shouts of joy rang in my heart. My sanity had been saved.

"Did you watch?" I asked.

With a sheepish grin he said, "I was prepped and ready to go. The nurse led me into the room. I took one look at what was happening and fainted dead away. I just came out of recovery myself.

I missed it all."

We almost named our little boy Christian, but in the end Pat thought that name was a bit too religious, so we settled on Christopher.

Russ and Susie came to see the new baby. When I laid Chris in Russ's arms, he gently caressed each one of his little fingers and toes, mesmerized by this tiny miracle. By the way he reacted, I wondered if he had ever seen a newborn before.

I was on maternity leave from my job and made plans to return to work as soon as possible. It was hard leaving little Christopher, but I needed that job for the sense of worth and gratification it gave me.

When I had first gone to work, I hired Wendy, a middle-aged woman with a family of her own, to be there when the girls got home from school and do light housework. Now, she became a full-time nanny and housekeeper. Not only that, she had daughters old enough to babysit in the evenings, if needed. My children grew to love Wendy and her girls like family.

For the next year or so, life settled into the semblance of a routine. Pat was doing his bookmaking thing and gone most of the time. He still had his temper tantrums, and we still walked on eggs when he was around.

For instance, I had a set of bowls with a strawberry design. It was one large bowl and six small matching bowls. Melissa, accidentally dropped and broke one of the smaller bowls on the Mexican tile kitchen floor. She felt really bad and started crying. I was consoling her and telling her it was okay, while Pat was yelling obscenities at her and treating her as if she had just committed a crime.

If the baby cried when Pat was home and trying to sleep, he would yell at me to "shut that fucking kid up." I learned to keep a blanket and pillow handy, so I could sleep on the floor next to Chris' crib, if necessary.

The girls were in school and thriving. I was back at my job. I had survived what I perceived as a crisis, and came out on the other side with the life-altering blessing of a son. Things weren't perfect by any means, but I was happy.

CHAPTER 17

CHRISTMAS 1978

Years of verbal abuse still made me timid and reluctant to approach Pat. Why was this so hard? Why do I have to be so fearful? Why couldn't we have a civil conversation about a normal subject?

"Dad called yesterday and my parents are talking about coming for a visit during Christmas." I had a hard time getting the words out.

"You mean just out of the blue? He snapped. "You must have invited them. What did you tell him?"

"I told him how wonderful. I told him I was ecstatic. It's been so long since they've seen the girls, and now we have a house with an extra bedroom for them."

"Goddammit, Joni, we can't have them staying here. It's a busy fucking time with playoffs and all that shit. It won't work. You should have asked me first."

I persevered. "You're working at Tommy's now, they won't

bother you."

"How long are they gonna be here?"

"They're talking about flying out Thursday before Christmas and flying back the next Thursday."

"Shit, that's way too long. They can get a fucking motel room."

This was important enough to me to persevere. "They shouldn't have to spend money on a motel room when we have a perfectly good place for them right here."

I knew better than to push any further. At least he didn't say they couldn't come. Maybe after he had some time to think about it, he would come around. Christmas was still a month away. The very thought of them being here made my heart feel all warm and tingly.

A few days later my sister, Carol, who lived in Redding, California with her husband Jack and their three boys, called. Six years older than I, we were never that close in childhood. However, after going through mom's near-death hospitalization together and now both raising a family, we had more in common.

"I talked to mom and dad and they said they were planning a trip to visit you at Christmas." She said.

"Yes, I can't wait, it's been so long since we've seen them." I answered.

"Well, Jack and I might drive down then too if that's okay." She replied.

"Sure, how fun to all be together for Christmas. We can meet your new baby and you can meet mine. Let's plan on it." She had just had her third boy last February and our Chris was born in May the year before.

The hard part was breaking the news to Pat.

"No fucking way. Goddammit, no FUCKING way. Don't they have a bunch of kids? Didn't you tell me she just had another fucking baby? How many is that? No, no, no. No fucking way."

We had just had our fourth child, she just had her third. What right did he have to judge? I stood my ground.

"Pat, it would mean everything to me to have all of us together. The cousins will have so much fun together. Carol and her family are coming Christmas Eve and leaving the day after Christmas so they won't be here long. They'll have to get a motel, so I'll just tell mom and dad they need to get one, too. I already told her yes, I can't call her back and tell her no."

Expecting more argument, I was surprised at his next comment.

"Well, last week, after you told me about your parents coming, I called Brian who has those new homes for sale at Palm Desert Country Club. I asked if there was a chance your parents could use one of the model homes for a week. He owes me big time and I told him he could pay off some of his debt this way and he agreed."

I couldn't believe what I was hearing. "Wow, those models are nice. How big are they?"

Reading my thought, he stated, "There's room enough for all

of the them. Thank god I'll be working most of the time."

What an answer to prayer. His selfish desire not to have my parents stay with us turned into a perfect option for everyone. "Thank you, Lord," I whispered.

The night before my parent's visit I tossed and turned. My heart was bursting with joy at the thought of seeing them again. But, as hard as I tried to suppress it, nightmarish details of their car accident ten years ago invaded my thoughts.

Please, no, I begged. Don't make me relive this again. But I couldn't turn off my mind and it went back to that tragic time of waiting for them to arrive, learning of their injuries, and the hospital in Iowa City.

Your mother may not make it through the night.

Tears filled my eyes and I could feel that empty hollow feeling in my stomach that I felt that day back in 1967. The vivid memories wouldn't go away. I got up for a glass of water hoping to break the spell. Through the starlit kitchen window, I gazed out at the sky. "God, please bring everyone here safely, I prayed. Take this anxiety from me." I felt His loving arms around me saying, "There, there, nothing's going to happen to them this time." I went back to bed and slept peacefully the rest of the night.

Dawn broke on a crisp and clear glorious Christmas Eve Day without a cloud in the sky. The girls were jumping up and down with excitement at the prospect of seeing grandma and grandpa. They had begged to go along to pick them up at the Palm Springs airport and I wouldn't have had it any other way.

With the backdrop of the snow-covered mountains, the sight of mom and dad stepping off that plane made my heart stop. I was frozen in my tracks by the wave of nostalgia that swept over me. I had no idea I missed them so much. The girls ran ahead to greet them, and the sight of mom and dad bending down to give them hugs took my breath away. I felt lightheaded, like I was going to faint. I couldn't speak. We briefly exchanged embraces on the tarmac, but I wanted to grab hold of them and never let go. The depth of my longing to have them in my life was overwhelming. I needed their warmth, their positive, enthusiastic nature, their unconditional love.

"How was your trip?" I asked.

"It was fine," Dad replied. "Wow, it is so good to see you, you look great! And these beautiful little girls look how they've grown. Let's see now, Tracy, you're the oldest. How old are you?"

"Eight."

"Well then that makes you seven, right Melissa?"

Melissa nodded her head.

Becky piped up, "I'm almost six!" Everyone laughed.

"It's so warm here," dad commented as he pulled his wool sweater off over his head. "We left Des Moines in twenty-degree weather and it's supposed to snow today. How warm do you think it is? Here, you girls can help me find our luggage."

The warmth of his enthusiastic chatter was music to my soul. Mom and I stood off to the side arm in arm. How good it felt to touch her. Our eyes locked for a moment, and I had to look away from those soft dark brown eyes as another wave of emotion swept through my entire being and my body shivered. My dear sweet mother!

On the drive back from the airport, mom and I chatted away in the front seat about plans for Christmas, while dad entertained the three girls in the back with I spy games. *He was never that much fun growing up, I mused.*

"Are Carol and Jack here yet?" Mom asked.

"They drove halfway down from Redding yesterday and should get here later today. By the way, Pat arranged for a house for you to stay in. It's a good-sized home with three bedrooms and two baths, plenty of room for you, Carol, Jack and the three boys. I can't wait to see the new baby."

"We have a whole house of our own?" Dad interjected. "What luxury."

"Did you bring your bathing suits?" I asked.

Mom laughed, "I had to dig mine out of a pile of items earmarked for the rummage sale at church. I haven't been swimming in so long. It's not very stylish and a bit snug, but will do in your back yard as long as nobody can see me."

"Well it took a few years, and I still can't believe I have a house with a pool," I gushed. "I vowed if I ever had my own pool I would swim laps every day and I do manage several days a week. I have to do it early in the morning, though, or it doesn't get done. This summer it was easy, but winter mornings are cold and dark. I am grateful for the heated water on cold winter mornings. It's not always easy to get out from under the warm covers, but I always feel so ready for the day after my invigorating swim."

"That's really great Joni, good for you." I savored the words of praise from dad.

"The guest list has grown for tomorrow." I continued.

"Oh, who all is coming?" Mom asked.

"Well, it will be our families which will be twelve right there.

Then, Pat's mother, brother and family makes sixteen and Russ and Susie, that makes eighteen. I can't wait for you to meet Pat's mother, I think you will really like her."

Carol and her family arrived safely and joined mom and dad at the model home. Christmas Day arrived warm and sunny. Having a crowd of family and friends for Christmas was the norm growing up. At last, it was my turn. Since we had invited Russ and Susie, and Pat's family was going to be there, he was obligated to stick around. I could feel that little quiver in the pit of my stomach as I pictured him being forced to interact with my family, but suppressed the feeling asking God to not let anything spoil this day.

The Christmas tree was aglow with multi colored lights, shiny ornaments, cranberry garlands and tinsel of silver. My tree had to be real and as tall as would fit in the room. I still wasn't used to Christmas in eighty-degree weather. The tree always seemed out of character without snow on the ground and a fire in the fireplace. A profusion of gifts spilled out from under the tree and grew larger as the guests arrived. The aroma of pine emanated into the room along with savory smells from the turkey roasting and pies baking in the oven.

Carol and I had visited mom and dad at the same time a couple of years earlier, so it wasn't like our kids had never seen one another, but they eyed each other warily and shyly upon greeting. It wasn't long, and they were chasing, teasing and playing as only cousins could do.

Once everyone arrived, presents were simultaneously being opened amidst the chaos of conversation, laughter and children darting in and out. Festive wrapping paper was strewn across the floor. There were smiles and comments as another mystery gift was revealed from inside a gaily-wrapped box and held up for all to see.

The t-shirts mom and dad gave each of the grandchildren, with their name emblazoned across the front were a big hit. The boys pulled off the shirts they were wearing and exchanged for the new. The girls put their shirts on right over their dresses. The sight of Keith, Melissa, Tracy, Benjy and Becky, aged eight to five, advertising their names was priceless. Chris and Curtis must have been deemed too small for t-shirts.

"Where's the camera?" I shouted. "We need to have a picture of these kids in their shirts."

From the leather couch came squeals of delight as dad played a tickle game from his childhood called Picky, Fisty, Flatty, Cutty, Clawy, with any child brave enough to come near. It was the same game he played with us when we were small.

As I gazed out across the room, and saw Carol visiting with Susie, heard mom laughing at something Pat's mom said and watched the children at play, peace and contentment washed over me. There was nothing like the love of my family.

"Lord, only You could pull this off." I prayed. "This is truly a Christmas miracle."

CHAPTER 18

HEMET

I was fixing breakfasts, packing lunches and reminding myself to tell the nanny a repairman was coming at 11:00, and wondering why Pat was still hanging around. He was usually long gone by now and there he still sat, reading the morning paper.

He spoke from his chair at the table, as I was at the sink putting dishes in the dishwasher, with Chris on one hip hoping his crankiness didn't mean he was coming down with a cold. "I bought a racehorse yesterday."

"Tracy help Becky find her other shoe," I demanded. "What, you bought a racehorse?" I asked incredulously. *So that's what's on his mind.*

"Yeah, Bill said it was a steal with great breeding. Some asshole needed the money."

"Who's Bill? You girls need to come eat your breakfast or we'll all be late." Chris was crying and rubbing his eyes, I felt his head to see if he had a temperature.

"He's a bookie friend of mine. He owns a horse ranch in Hemet and really knows his stuff when it comes to horses."

"Where's Hemet?" I asked, looking at the clock and realizing I still needed to get myself dressed. "What are you going to do with a racehorse?"

"It's a thoroughbred, I'll fucking race it." He sneered, his voice full of sarcasm.

Just then the doorbell rang. *Thank God for Wendy.* I handed Chris to her as she entered, and she immediately took over with the children.

I walked over to where Pat was sitting, "Doesn't it cost a lot of money to own a horse?"

I thought back to when I was young, playing cowboys and Indians with my brother on the farm, and dreaming of having my own horse. We already had a barn with hay bales in the loft. I couldn't understand why I couldn't have a horse. When I begged for

257

one, dad went into a big lecture on how expensive it was to own a horse.

"Yeah, but it's going to make money winning races. Bill's boarding it in exchange for money he owes me."

Glancing at the clock again, now, I realized I really was going to be late.

"Well, if you already bought it there isn't much I can say. I need to get to work."

As I hurried down the hall he called out, "I'm driving over there to see the horse on Friday, do you want to go with me?"

Still trying to digest what he told me, late for work and now he wants me to commit to driving to Hemet on the weekend? "Sure, I guess so," I hastily called back, not really sure just how I felt.

With that, he was out the door.

A thoroughbred racehorse, what next, the man is insane.

I had time to think as I drove to work. The thought of owning a horse was exciting. It was nice that he wanted me to go with him to see the horse. He did say he had a place to keep it and someone to look after it, so it probably wouldn't impact us too much.

On Saturday morning, we set out for Hemet to see the horse. I wished the kids were with us, but Pat wouldn't have been able to tolerate it. Furthermore, I would have been tense, fearing they would do something to set him off.

This little burg was off the beaten path, and not on the way to anywhere, yet in the heart of Southern California. Bill's horse ranch was on the outskirts of town. It was like stepping into another world. The ranch was bigger than I thought it was going to be with acres and acres of fenced off pastureland. The barn was gigantic with stall after stall lining both sides of the hey-strewn walkway. The aroma of the fresh hay and stable smells was intoxicating. Bill led us through the maze of dirt paths that separated each grazing area. I had never seen so many beautiful horses! We stopped. Bill leaned over the rail, gave a whistle, and a beast of a horse trotted over to where we stood. The massive size of this animal took my breath away.

The two men were deep in conversation about plans they had in regard to this horse. I heard, Del Mar, Santa Anita, Los Alamitos, and figured these must be race tracks. Bill was savvy about the business and Pat was like a sponge absorbing as much knowledge as he could.

When we got back in the car for the return trip, Pat's mind was going a mile a minute. The excitement of actually seeing the horse and hearing of the potential for greatness captivated him. "Joni, I think we should move to Hemet so we can be near the horse. Let's look at houses for sale before we leave."

Move?! Move to Hemet? Are you kidding me? I could never leave Palm Desert. What about schools? What about my job? What about friends? I'm finally adjusting to life where I live and now you want to uproot me?

"Well, I don't mind driving through town just to see it, but move here? That's pretty drastic just because of a horse." I said to placate him.

"Yes, but I can work from anywhere and I really want to get

involved in the horse business. It has always been a dream of mine. This is a golden opportunity to learn from the best."

Driving through the streets of Hemet as we talked, I was struck by the rural feel reminding me of my childhood. Florida Avenue was one long street from end to end, with the downtown limited to six or eight blocks. The east end of Florida Avenue became the highway that went up and over the mountains to Palm Desert. We spotted a couple of restaurants that looked like they could be decent, but that was about it. Most of the homes we passed were modest, older single level bungalows, too small for our family of six.

"These homes are pathetic," Pat said with distain

Oh good, maybe this will discourage him from wanting to live in Hemet.

As he spoke, we turned onto Cornell Street, reminding me of my high school friend, Cathy Cornell. I was deep in thought reminiscing about my high school days when he shouted out, "Hey, there's a for sale sign."

I looked up to see a very large home set back from the street. It was on a corner and appeared to take up at least two lots.

"Come on," he insisted, as he pulled over to the curb in front of the home. "Let's go look at it."

The front yard was big enough for a game of football, divided by a stone path leading from the street to the front door.

"Let's go this way." Pat grabbed my hand and led me around to the side of the house.

"Wow, look at those roses," I exclaimed as we passed by a large garden full of every kind of rose imaginable.

I couldn't believe my eyes when we got around back. There was an upper level yard near the house, with a small fishpond and stone steps leading down to a beautiful green lawn on the lower level. The back of the house wrapped around a huge oak tree with a raised red brick tree ring at the base.

"That tree is huge!" I exclaimed.

"Look at this fucking place, the lower level would be perfect for my office." Pat said.

Each new discovery was more exciting than the last. The home was gorgeous and the yard would be an excellent place for the kids to play.

"Pat, it's beautiful and huge! It looks a bit tired though. The paint is peeling off the trim and some of the brickwork is crumbling. The whole house could use a paint job."

"We can fix it up." I could hear the enthusiasm in his voice.

We walked up a cement ramp on the backside of the home that opened up to a large cemented area suitable for a basketball court. The garage was separated from the house by a trellised walkway. At one time it was probably beautiful, but now the vines were overgrown and unruly.

"Oh my gosh," I said in a whisper, "what a great place to raise a family. I might even be convinced to move if I could live in a home like this."

Pat jotted down the phone number written on the hand-made

for sale sign, and we headed home continuing to talk about the house.

"How many bedrooms do you think it has?" I asked.

"Probably four, maybe five counting the master bedroom, then there's the whole fucking downstairs."

"The kitchen was so cute and the breakfast nook with the big floor to ceiling windows facing the back yard, how cool. That laundry room is as big as a bedroom and it has windows all around." I could picture myself there.

"How about the living room, it was hard to see in, but it has to be huge and it has a real brick fireplace." Pat added.

The conversation was exhilarating. I sat close to Pat as we talked.

"We'd have to have a full-time gardener to maintain the grounds. That would be expensive."

"Joni quit fucking worrying about the money. We can afford a gardener."

"Yes, but we have no way of knowing what they might be asking for this place. I'm sure we can't afford it. We shouldn't get our hopes up. Besides, whatever the price, we would have to get a loan and we have no credit established or money in a bank."

"You just let me fucking worry about the money. You're just looking for a fucking excuse. You're always so goddamn worried and fearful. I don't know how you accomplish anything. What ails you?"

I had set him off, dwelling too much on the money. It was my fault.

I sank back in the seat and moved closer to the passenger door. We rode in silence the rest of the way.

Maybe this would be good for our little family. Could I possibly get past the ugliness of the past and move toward a renewed relationship with my husband? I'm willing to try, but don't know if I can put my trust in him. Sometimes he seems to want the family life, but then spoils it with some rash behavior.

We were greeted with enthusiasm by our beautiful children as we walked through the door. *Would they be better off raised in the small-town atmosphere of Hemet?* Suddenly, our home I was so excited about four years ago, felt small and ordinary.

Later that evening, Pat called the number on the for sale sign, while I busied myself with the routine of getting the children settled in for the night. Thirty minutes later he was still on the phone.

What could they be talking about for so long? Might there be a possibility? We haven't even discussed this in depth with each other. Who am I kidding we never discuss anything in depth. Pat just makes up his mind and we do it. The price will probably be way out of our range and that will be the end of it. Is he making some sort of crazy promise that we can't possibly keep?

"Okay, Paul, I'll call you tomorrow." Pat hung up the phone.

"That was a long conversation, who were you talking to?"

"The fucking owner of the house, that's who. His name is Paul Howard. He and his family owned The Howard Rose Company in Hemet, which explains the rose garden. He built the house for his

266

family back in the early 40's and said it was the finest home in Hemet at the time."

"So, how much is he asking for it?"

"$250,000."

The tension in my stomach eased a bit. We could never afford that much.

"I told him that was more than we could afford. Then, he asked about our family and why we wanted to move to Hemet. I told him the story."

Did you tell him we haven't even discussed this between us yet?

"Then he told me the home has been on the market for almost two years without a serious offer. Just recently his wife was admitted to a home and he has no use for it anymore, he just wants to get rid of it. He sounded desperate and asked me to make an offer."

"Did you offer something?"

"I told him I had to discuss it with you and would get back to him."

"What about the fact that we would have to get a loan?"

"That's the fucking beauty of it all, he is willing to carry the papers. Can you fucking believe it?

"How much would you offer for it?"

"Hell, we have nothing to lose and I think he's vulnerable. I may as well go low. I think I'll offer $175,000."

"He'll never go for that," I laughed. *I'd move if we could buy it for that.*

The following night, Pat called Paul back with the offer of $175,000. Without hesitation Paul accepted.

The lure of this new adventure overshadowed everything else. I rationalized away my objections. With the money Pat was making we really did not need my income. My job was an escape route. Maybe this was God telling me I needed to quit thinking about an escape route and start trusting in the future with my husband. The kids needed their mother at home, and if we moved, I wouldn't work.

I would enjoy that. Maybe this was a steppingstone for us.

I needed to put the dark memories of the past behind me. There really was only that one time that Pat became physically abusive. Alcohol was the trigger and maybe with continued sobriety his anger issues will subside.

The school year was ending and we could make the move over the summer. At ages 8, 7, 5 and 2, none of them were old enough to be too traumatized by the change.

On July 19, 1979, I drove to Hemet with a load of our personal belongings. The kids and I spent our first night in our new home camped out in sleeping bags. Pat stayed behind to supervise the loading of the van the following day.

Pat hired TK and Linda, a professional interior design team, to completely redo every room in our house. He allowed each of our girls to choose the color scheme for their own rooms, Tracy chose yellow, Melissa chose pink and Becky chose navy blue. We had Chris' room all done in denim and plaids for a boy, but at two years of age he was too scared to sleep there alone.

The kitchen cabinets were painted a steely blue with gray slate tiles on the floor. The living room walls were done in a padded floral fabric.

French doors were added to the master bedroom leading to the balcony overlooking the back yard.

A cement walkway and gazebo were added to the lower yard.

The entire outside of the home and trim was painted.

The downstairs was re-carpeted with the best Berber carpet money could buy and furnished with leather couches and hunter green accents for a very masculine look.

The following year, when it was all completed, the garden club of Hemet included our home on their annual home tour. It was truly a showpiece.

My immediate task upon arriving in Hemet, was to get Tracy, Melissa and Becky enrolled in school for the fall.

Sitting in the multi-purpose room of Little Lake Elementary

for the new parent welcome orientation, fond memories of my elementary years filled my senses.

I could see the rows of desks in the classroom, the playground with its giant strides and swings and the auditorium where we square danced. I could smell the combination of chalk dust, janitorial disinfectant and sweaty bodies just in from recess. I could hear the teacher's stern voice settling us down and the rustle of desks opening as paper, pencils and books were retrieved from inside. I loved the feel of the No. 2 pencil in my hand and the way the soft lead transferred onto the lined paper of my Big Chief tablet as I wrote.

I would have been a good elementary school teacher. My love of learning, coupled with my love of children, was a perfect match. Well, I had no degree. The opportunity was right in front of me and I turned my back on it – twice.

My thoughts were interrupted when I heard the principal talking about the PTA and how they were always looking for parent volunteers. The more she talked the more I knew this was for me.

I joined Little Lake Elementary PTA and became president the following year. I served in some capacity from 1979 – 1988 until we had no more children attending that school.

Pat never set foot inside the school.

Tracy, Melissa and Becky had been part of the Piranhas swim team in Indio, and I enrolled them in the highly competitive Dolphin Swim Club in Hemet. I became President of the club and cherished the friends I made.

We joined Soboba Country Club. The girls and I took tennis lessons and went to the club pool on hot summer days. I joined the women's tennis group and played in tournaments. Pat wanted nothing to do with any of our activities or any of my friends. He considered them all beneath him.

Pat did provide us with a memorable family vacation to Nine

Quarter Circle Ranch near Yellowstone Park in Montana, a storybook experience.

We stayed in one of the authentic log cabins spread out from the main lodge. An age-old dinner bell called us to family style hearty meals.

Each of us picked out a horse that would be ours for the duration of the stay.

We went on trail rides hiked and fished.

In the evenings there was square dancing in a huge barn, hayrides and outdoor cookouts under the stars.

Tracy, Melissa and Becky learned how to ride and took part in a rodeo competition at the end of the stay.

At three years of age, Chris was too young to participate in much, but there were staff babysitters available whenever we wanted to do something on our own.

Pat wanted me to experience fly-fishing, so we hired a guide to take us to the Snake River where we donned waders and trekked out into the swift waters. We laughed and frolicked in the icy waters, delighting in the shared experience.

I relaxed and let down my guard. *Why couldn't our lives together be like this more often?* I really wanted us to get along. I wanted our family to stay together. If only I could trust him, but I had been demeaned and downtrodden too many times, and I knew it was just a matter of time before his ugly side would surface.

Pat was in his own world of gambling and horses. Occasionally, he would take the family out to the horse ranch to see the thoroughbreds. The kids enjoyed it, but the horses couldn't be ridden, so their interest waned. We ended up owning three different horses that won races, Fayre Spin, Leckie and Tiburon.

When Pat got involved with the horses he connected with his first son, Kevin, aged 21, living in Pennsylvania and invited him and his girlfriend to come live with us and work on the ranch.

As usual, we didn't discuss it, but I was in favor of Kevin and his girlfriend coming, because family was important to me and I

274

thought it would be good for them to establish a relationship.

On July 2, 1982 Leckie won at Del Mar racetrack in Del Mar, California with Willie Shoemaker riding. Our entire family including Kevin and Sue, dressed in our finest, stood in the winner's circle celebrating the win. Del Mar, the summer playground for Bing Crosby and many celebrity stars. Del Mar, small and quaint with its Spanish Colonial architectural style. Del Mar, the backdrop for horses from Seabiscuit to Cigar. Del Mar where jockeys with names like Johnny Longden, Willie Shoemaker and Laffit Pincay, Jr. were legend.

Sue was a sweetheart, but Pat and Kevin clashed from the start. Kevin's expectation was, Pat owed him and Pat's expectation was, Kevin needed to prove himself through hard work at the ranch. Neither of them was interested in living up to either expectation. Nor were they interested in working at being close as father and son. Many days, when they came home from the stables, they either weren't speaking or they were yelling obscenities at each other. Pat told him the familiar words, "If you don't want to work you should go back to fucking Pennsylvania where you belong." It took a couple of years, but that's exactly what he ended up doing.

Years later, we received tragic news. Kevin had fallen asleep smoking a cigarette and burned to death in the fire. He was living with his mother and she received severe burns on her hands and face attempting to save him. The news was devastating. Pat never spoke about it.

CHAPTER 19

THE FINAL STRAW

It was a gorgeous fall Saturday, sunny, bright and beautiful and our third year in Hemet. The warmth and vitality I always felt after a morning of playing tennis at Soboba Country Club was still with me. My muscles felt toned and I knew I looked good in my cute little white one-piece tennis dress and deep tan. Working up a good sweat was always good for my soul.

I gathered up the kids from the pool, and stopped by the grocery store on the way home. We were all famished and looking forward to tuna salad sandwiches for lunch, everyone's favorite. What a joy these children were! Their youth and enthusiasm were contagious and I never tired of their banter and chatter. Tracy, the pensive and practical oldest child, Melissa, carefree and confident, Becky, full of life and Christopher, all boy, were the light of my life.

We pulled into the garage and the kids piled out.

"Hey, Tracy and Melissa," I shouted. "Help me with these

bags."

I juggled my purse and groceries, trying to make it all in one trip. Chris and Becky frolicked up ahead. Suddenly, we stopped dead in our tracks. At the door were two police officers in full uniform. One was a tall imposing man, standing off to the side and the other, a chunky, buxom woman, was sitting on the stoop. Their demeanor implied they had been there for a while. I hadn't noticed the police car in front of the house when I drove in.

The female officer stood, and holding out an official looking document growled, "I have a warrant for the arrest of Thomas Patrick McCormick."

"He isn't here," I replied, trying to keep my voice calm and steady.

She then produced another official looking document and stated, "This is a search warrant and authorizes us to search your home."

With hands shaking, I unlocked the door and let them in.

Tracy headed down the hall toward her bedroom.

"Not so fast," the female officer demanded. "You all need to stay together while we conduct our search."

"Can I at least put away my groceries? I have ice cream that will melt," I pleaded.

She shot me a menacing glance and reluctantly replied, "Go ahead, but be quick."

As I moved around the kitchen from the refrigerator to the cupboards and back, there were four little bodies hovering around me. "It's okay," I spoke consolingly even though I was scared, too.

Once I finished, the female officer pointed to the living room and said, "Stay together, in there."

I kept reassuring the kids everything was going to be all right, we just needed to let them do their search and it would soon be over. My mind was reeling. I had received a phone call a few days earlier from a family friend who owned the local newspaper and whose children were on the same swim team as ours. He said, "I shouldn't be doing this, and I won't be able to keep it out of the newspaper when it happens, but the police are planning a raid of your home soon. I can't tell you exactly the day, but as a courtesy to a friend I wanted to warn you."

When I told Pat about the phone call, he decided it would be best if he went to the desert and worked out of Tommy's apartment for a few days.

They probably weren't going to find much evidence because Pat kept most of his paperwork in a briefcase he carried with him. If he had been here and working it would have been a different story.

What if they arrest me! Would they consider me an accomplice? What would they do with the children? I couldn't let myself think that way. I had to stay positive and strong. What was taking them so long?

"Do you have the key to the cupboards downstairs?" The officer asked from the doorway.

"Yes," I replied. "I'll get it."

I was allowed to leave the living room and get the key, much to the chagrin of the children. They didn't want me to leave their side. An hour and a half later, both officers came back to the kitchen. They had a few incidental items in their hands, but were probably disappointed with their findings.

Now what? Would they come put me in handcuffs and take me away? Still dressed in my tennis outfit, I felt drops of sweat sliding down the middle of my back.

The female officer came to the living room and announced, "You can come out now, we're through." With that, they turned and walked out the back door.

I could breathe again. Tears of relief welled up in my eyes, but I held them at bay. I went straight to the phone and dialed Pat's number in the desert. *Had they put a wiretap on the phone?* I should probably be careful what I say.

"The police just left here," I blurted out. My voice an octave higher than normal.

"They were?" he replied in a calm measured tone.

"YES!" I wailed. "They made us all stay in the living room for hours, while they searched the house."

All Pat said was, "Did they find anything?"

"I don't think so, just a couple of notebooks is all."

"Good, there isn't much there to find. Okay, gotta go." He hung up.

Wait a minute! What about me? What about the kids? Is that all you have to say? Don't you realize the emotional turmoil we have just been through? How about "I'm sorry you had to experience that" or something, anything.

I thought about how good life in Hemet was for me and the children. I was becoming my own person and it felt good. I had learned to suppress my negative feelings towards my husband and ignore his narcissistic ways. The trouble was, these feelings were always brewing just below the surface. Why did I keep pretending everything was fine when it wasn't?

It had been a long time since I had cried over his behavior. I cried so many tears in the past, I finally stopped shedding tears. Lying awake in bed that night I wanted to cry, but the tears wouldn't come.

Just past 10:00 p.m. I heard noises in the kitchen and Pat came hurriedly into the bedroom.

"Oh my gosh, you scared me!" I cried out.

He didn't respond.

"What are you doing?" I asked.

Still, he didn't say a word as he pulled an overnight bag from the closet and began throwing items in it. "I'll call you," he whispered as he headed out the door. He wasn't there more than ten minutes.

I lay awake all night contemplating my life and the lives of our children. This man and I had pieced together an existence that was a farce. He didn't really care about me and I didn't really care about him. This was no way to live. The children and I were home alone ninety percent of the time as it was, and his presence only disrupted our lives. We all walked on eggs when he was around, and were relieved when he was gone. Tracy, Melissa and Becky were happy, healthy, contented children who enjoyed life. I worried about Chris, as a boy, and the negative impact this man would have on his life. He was five years old and I needed to protect him from his own father.

I didn't hear from Pat for several days, and figured he had gone back to the desert. When the phone rang, I didn't care if it was him or not.

"Hi, it's me," came his voice from the other end of the line. "You'll never fucking guess where I am." Without waiting for an answer, he continued, "I'm in fucking Oklahoma! I'm at Don Mathis' ranch."

Who was Don Mathis?

"It is a beautiful horse ranch. You can't believe how big it is! Don owns hundreds of thoroughbreds and thousands of acres of land it's incredible! I'm staying in his guesthouse and it's huge! There's plenty of room here for all of us. Don said we could use it as long as we need it. Joni, I really want you and the kids to move down here with me. We could have a great life here on the ranch. They have good schools and . . .

I interrupted him mid-sentence. "Pat, no."

Now it was his turn to be silent.

"It's over. I can't believe you would expect us to disrupt our lives once again. After three years the girls are well established in a good school with great friends and great neighbors. They are excelling on the swim team. Chris will be in first grade in the fall. I have responsibilities and have developed great friendships in this community. It's obvious you have no regard for any of us. All you think about is yourself. I'd rather go it alone with these four children than keep putting up with your demands and abuses. I don't know what your plans are, but we are not moving to Oklahoma."

The minute these words were out of my mouth, I knew I had

made the right decision.

CHAPTER 20

STAYING SANE

As the months rolled by, money became a big issue. Pat sent money sporadically at first and we made it through the holiday's, but when he could see that I was serious about not moving to Oklahoma, the payments dwindled.

There wasn't much money left in our bank account, so I figured out which bills were absolutely necessary and ignored the rest. The house payment was the biggest chunk and would buy me the most time. I was counting on Paul Howard to give me some time to figure things out.

It was a gorgeous day in March. The red tulips that lined the front of the house were in full bloom. The air was warm and smelled of flowers and spring. I was wearing shorts and a tee shirt, my favorite attire.

I walked to the mailbox out by the street to get the mail, and as I headed back toward the house I began casually flipping through the stack of mail. About halfway through, I saw the return address of Paul Howard on one of the envelopes.

Fearing the worst, the reality of my situation hit me. An intense wave of fear came over me, my knees buckled and I sank to the ground. The mail dropped out of my hands and scattered on the ground around me. The world started spinning and I blacked out for a few seconds.

What just happened? I couldn't move and wasn't sure if I could get up. I groveled on my hands and knees, gathering up the strewn pieces of mail. I stood up, looking around hoping no one had seen me and made my way inside the house. Closing the door, I stood leaning against it, holding on to the knob, fearing that I would fall again. Sweat was pouring out of me. I needed help. Frantic, I got in my car and drove to the home of friends I had met through the swim team. I burst into their home without warning, sobbing hysterically. I couldn't catch my breath or speak. I thought I was dying.

The startled couple didn't know what to do. They were on

the verge of calling for help when I slowly began to gain my composure. I told my story and they listened.

Realizing my immediate need was money, Larry said he would help me find a job. He calmly talked about how dire it seemed now, but step by step things would get better. Kathy told me I could call any time day or night if I needed to talk.

By the time I left, over an hour later, I was feeling much better. Larry gave me his gasoline credit card to use for as long as I needed it. As I was leaving he gave me $1,000 in cash and said not to worry about paying it back. I was overwhelmed by their generosity.

The swim team was like one big family and it didn't take long for me to find a job once the word got out.

The next looming task was to file for divorce and get that ball rolling for child support and alimony. Another Dolphin Swim Team parent was an attorney. I made an appointment with him. I nervously walked into his office with my box of paperwork.

"Sit down, Joni," he motioned to the chair across the desk from him.

"Thanks. Where do you want this box?"

"I'll take that home with me and look through it, but let's talk a bit about your situation."

"Well, as you know we have four children and a house here in Hemet. We also still own a home in Palm Desert. My husband makes his living as a bookie, so he has money, but it is not traceable. Our home here in Hemet was raided by the police a few weeks ago and he fled to Oklahoma. He wants me to come there with the children, but I am not going to go. We have too much invested here in Hemet. I like this town and the children and I have established ourselves here. The marriage has been tumultuous over the years and I just want out."

"I'll take a look at the paperwork you've brought me and get back to you tomorrow."

He called the next day. "Could you come back to my office this afternoon?"

"Sure," I replied. Wondering why he needed to see me again so soon.

When I arrived at his office, the box I had brought to him the day before was sitting on the corner of his desk.

"Joni, I went through your paperwork last night and I'm afraid you need someone with a bit more expertise than I can provide. This could get complicated and I don't think I'm equipped to handle it. I'm so sorry."

I didn't know what to say. "Do you have anyone you could recommend?"

"Frankly, I don't think there is anyone in town that can handle it. You're probably going to have to go out of the area to find someone."

What a blow. I wanted to scream, *How can you turn me down? I need your help.* But instead, I stood, lifted the box of papers off his desk and walked out.

I was trying to stay positive, but the job I secured at The Hemet News didn't pay much and I didn't know where to turn next on securing an attorney. These things were preying on my mind, and at the PTA meeting the following week I had a hard time concentrating on the agenda I had prepared as President.

At the end of the meeting, one of the Board members, a prominent leader of the community, came up to me. "You seemed a bit preoccupied tonight, Joni, is everything okay?"

"Wow, I didn't realize it was that obvious," I answered. I glanced over at him hoping his concern was genuine.

"I understand you are dealing with some personal issues. It must be hard."

"You know, in many ways, it is actually easier and I try not to worry too much. I just want to get on with my life. Last week I went to an attorney here in town to start divorce proceedings, and to my amazement he turned me down. He said my issues were too complicated for him to handle and I would probably need to go out of the area to find someone with that kind of expertise. I'm at a loss as to what to do next."

"I deal with attorneys all the time in my business. The law firm I use is in Riverside. Maybe I can help. Do you want me to see what I can do?"

"Sure, that would be great. Thank you so much."

Lying in bed that night I thought about his offer. Who was I kidding? An experienced Riverside attorney was bound to be expensive and I had no money.

A few days later he called. "I have an attorney for you."

"You do?"

"Yes, his name is Ed Mackey. He works for a law firm by the name of Swarner & Fitzgerald in downtown Riverside. Give his office a call and set up an appointment. His secretary knows you'll be calling."

"He must be expensive."

"You'll have to discuss money with him, but I know he'll be fair."

"Well, I just don't want to waste his time if I can't afford him."

"Just make the call."

I pulled into the parking structure on the appointed day in downtown Riverside. The building was several stories high. I found Swarner & Fitzgerald on the directory – 6B. Once inside the elevator I sat my box down while I pushed the button for the sixth floor. What would he be like? Would he be tall or short? Would he be ugly, fat, good looking? Would he be all business? What if I hand him my box of papers and he takes one look and says he can't help me? What about his fees? Any amount would be too much for me with no money. Why did I agree to this? Ding! Sixth floor, time to get out.

The door to the front lobby area of 6B opened at the center of a spacious room. To the far right were a few waiting room chairs under high windows. To the far left, a woman sat behind a large dark mahogany desk with stacks and stacks of books behind her on floor to ceiling dark wood bookshelves. This plump, professionally dressed woman came out from behind her desk and greeted me with a friendly smile.

"You must be Joni," she said in a warm caring voice.

"Here, give me that box, it must have been heavy to carry all the way up here." She reminded me of a favorite second grade school teacher I had. Little did I know she would be the one I would end up dealing with the most for the next several months.

We hadn't exchanged many words, when the door to Ed Mackey's office opened and he beckoned for me to come in. He wasn't what I was expecting at all. He was a very slight built man, not too tall wearing glasses. His mannerisms were those of someone whose time was valuable. Other than acknowledging that his good friend referred me to him, and he was happy to help the friend of a friend, he was all business. I couldn't decide if he was just extremely busy or perhaps a bit shy, but he gave no indication of giving me my box back and sending me on my way.

"Before we start I need to talk to you about your fees." I blurted out. "I don't have any money and don't know how I am going to pay you. I do have a job, but it doesn't pay much."

"I appreciate your concern and honesty so let's talk about money. I usually ask my clients for a retainer fee, you know, some money up front, but because of our mutual friend, that won't be necessary. I charge by the hour for my time, but by having my secretary handle as much as possible her time is less expensive. I don't want you to have to drive from Hemet any more than necessary so we will keep office visits to a minimum.

Another big expense will be court room time. It's hard to predict that now, but let me assure you I will be thoroughly prepared when the time comes and I don't tolerate delay tactics and shenanigans in court. I have a good reputation and judges know I am a straight shooter. Let's talk about how much you think you can afford to pay me each month and we'll start there. Whatever figure we agree to you can just pay monthly from now until it all gets paid off. How does that sound?"

"That sounds more than fair. Thank you so much." *Maybe this will work.*

"Well, you and Rose need to get acquainted. She has a client form that needs to be filled out and will be asking you some questions. I saw the box sitting on her desk which I will go through. Going forward most of my communication with you will be through her. Don't worry, she's been with me for years and knows what to do. I have to be in court shortly, so unless you have any other questions at this time I'll leave you to her."

True to his word on May 28, 1985 Ed Mackey stamped his seal on the paperwork and I was a divorced woman for the second time, $10,000 in debt. Pat was ordered to pay child support of $350 per month per child until the age of eighteen. He was granted the Hemet house and I was granted the Palm Desert house.

True to my word, I continued to make our agreed upon monthly payments until two years later, when I was able to pay off the balance of my commitment to the attorney through the sale of the desert home.

I stayed in Hemet and raised my four children as a single parent. They were some of the best years of our lives.

CHAPTER 21

FORGIVENESS

I answered the phone with my usual, "Hello?"

"Hi, Joni?" My body tensed. This voice from the past I would have recognized under any circumstance.

"Yes," I cautiously responded.

It was 2005 and my ex-husband was close to death. My first thought when I heard Davy's voice was he was calling to tell me Pat had passed away. The children were there with him though. One of them would have called if this were true.

"It's Davey Evans," he said. "Pat wanted me to call you."

I could tell from a slight quaver in his voice that he was nervous. I hadn't spoken to Davey in years. He spoke quickly, avoiding small talk. This was out of character as Davey was ordinarily an incessant talker.

"He wants you to come here, he wants to see you."

A few days earlier, when my oldest daughter informed me

that hospice had been called in I contemplated going there but quickly dismissed the idea. I didn't want to be where I might not be welcome. Twenty years had passed since our divorce. I had seen Pat in the interim, when occasions warranted it, but each encounter had been strained and uncomfortable.

My initial reaction to Davey's request was a resounding no. Why would I want to go there and subject myself to whatever tongue-lashing or ridicule might be awaiting? What negative spin was he going to put on the conversation? Verbal abuse was his expertise.

"I know this is probably not something you want to do, and I don't blame you, but this is his dying request and I said I would call you." Davey continued.

I immediately began to conjure up excuses. It's a two-hour drive. What would my current husband say? I needed to be at work.

Conversely, it would be nice to be there with the children. We could be each other's moral support.

How could I deny a dying man's final request?

Davey broke the silence. "I need to give him an answer. Will you come?"

Setting my fears and reservations aside, I finally spoke. "I'll come."

"It needs to be tomorrow, there isn't much more time," Davey urged, "Can you come tomorrow?"

"Yes," I replied.

We both hung up without saying goodbye.

Pat and his girlfriend, Sandy, lived together in Palm Desert. I had visited there in the past, so knew where to go. She was a ditsy redhead and from the stories my son, who lived with them for a while would tell, she was crazy. According to him, they fought non-stop.

I gathered my courage at the door and was ushered in by

one of the guests. Their home had a very open floor plan with a large living/family room area. Several long-time friends had already gathered and were casually sitting around the room visiting among themselves. I recognized most of them. Some were familiar enough to recall their names, while others I knew, but couldn't put a name to a face. There was the occasional sound of laughter as familiar stories were told. Stories that had been told a hundred times before were being repeated as if for the first time.

Pat was propped up in a hospital bed on the far side of the room. Sandy, relishing in her role as hostess to those who had come to pay their last respects was playing the part of the attentive wife. She lit a cigarette for Pat and placed it between his lips so he could take a long drag. When he got distracted while the cigarette burned down in the ashtray, she lit another one and gave it to him. In between puffs on the cigarettes she held a glass of wine up to his lips and gave him a sip. Since the end was near, she was giving him whatever he wanted.

The scene was reminiscent of his favorite pastime throughout the years. Sitting in a bar with all his cronies around, swapping stories, smoking cigarettes and drinking. He was in his element.

As I walked in, all heads turned toward me, and the room suddenly became quiet. Sandy put down the unlit cigarette and glass of wine, and scurried into the kitchen.

Pat saw me across the room, and motioned for me to come over. I walked across the room and stopped by his bedside. I stood there, not knowing what to expect or what to say. He looked directly at me and softly whispered, "Thank you for coming." He patted the edge of the bed with his frail, weak hand and in a raspy voice said, "Sit here beside me."

Up close, I could see how dreadfully pale and thin he was. Yet, there was a calm about him I had never witnessed before. He seemed at peace with his circumstance. He had always been such an agitated, nervous, antsy person that I didn't recognize this demeanor. I held back a bit, still not comfortable with what might transpire.

With effort, he spoke again. "It's okay. Sit down. I want to talk to you."

I gingerly sat down on the edge of the bed.

"I asked you to come to tell you I'm sorry. I'm sorry for everything I put you through."

Stunned, I searched his face for the telltale signs of anger roiling beneath the surface ready to erupt at any moment. In all the time I knew him, he had never uttered the words I'm sorry. Years of alcoholism, years of womanizing, years of gambling and years of verbal and physical abuse had all been defended, twisted, denied, ignored, but never acknowledged. Tears welled up in my eyes. "It's okay," I managed to say. "It was a long time ago."

"No, it's not okay," he continued. "I need you to know I'm truly sorry and I'm asking for your forgiveness."

The gaze of his faded, tired eyes never left my face. Pat never spoke of his faith, but something told me God compelled him to do this. Perhaps Pat thought it would help him get into heaven, and maybe it would. Whatever the motive, he was sincere, and I knew what I needed to do.

"I forgive you," I managed, in a voice choked with emotion, as the tears spilled over and ran down my face.

He started crying too. I leaned forward and we embraced.

Something supernatural occurred in that moment. God lifted a monumental weight from my shoulders.

Two days later, I stood alone at the gravesite. A warm gentle desert breeze ruffled my hair, the kind of mesmerizing breeze I never knew existed growing up in the muggy mid-west.

Memories darted around in my head as scenes that had lain dormant were resurrected, triggered by eulogies at the service earlier. We had divorced long ago, but part of me felt like the grieving widow. We had been married fourteen years and borne four children together. Didn't that count for something?

Prior to the brief ceremony in the chapel, the children and I had walked down the aisle together and stood in silence, beside the open casket, gazing down, with our arms around each other. I had no way of knowing what was going through each of my children's minds, but the thought that struck me was, finally he has no more power over any of us. Just when I began to think no one was going to speak, quietly Chris said, "He was an interesting man." The girls and I nodded in agreement. After another minute or two, we turned and walked back up the aisle.

Only a handful of people came to the gravesite to witness the internment. It had been a long time since I attended a funeral with an open casket and burial, and this brought back its own set of memories from childhood.

As people began to gather around the gravesite, I noticed a woman dressed in black standing some distance away, as if she didn't want to intrude. The graveside ceremony was brief and I felt a sense of relief when it was over. As I turned and headed toward the car, the woman in black walked toward me.

Who was this stranger?

She extended her hand for me to shake, and with a voice full of warmth and enthusiasm, like an old dear friend, she gushed, "Hi Joni."

I searched the depths of this thin, wrinkle-lined face with the deep-set eyes, but there was no recognition.

Sensing this, she spoke again, "It's me, Jerry."

Still, nothing.

"Jerry, Jerry Cheney."

Slowly, slowly the years began to peel away, layer by layer, until a very pretty, much younger face emerged before me.

Jerry Cheney, the woman I suspected of being with my husband all those years ago.

What had compelled her to attend his funeral? Had they gotten together again after our divorce?

When I realized who she was, there was no thought of anger

or bitterness. Instead, I was overcome with a strange sense of sadness and compassion for this woman. I placed both my hands over hers and gave it a warm gentle squeeze.

"Oh my, Jerry, it's been a long time hasn't it? It's good to see you."

Forgiveness is freedom.

EPILOGUE

The events in my story began over fifty years ago. Yet, it feels like only yesterday.

When I finally said no to uprooting my family from California to Oklahoma, I began my journey of becoming the real me for the first time since childhood.

As a child I was loved, carefree and happy. My upbringing was idealistic.

My earthly father was a stern taskmaster, but in a healthy way. We were expected to behave, and if we didn't, there was punishment. It is my opinion that he, innocently, emphasized punishment over forgiveness.

When I learned that I had sinned in a big way at age fourteen, I was certain I was doomed to spend eternity in hell. I spent my teenage years devotedly faithful to my boyfriend, and breathed a sigh of relief when we finally married at age nineteen, hoping that would save me.

The year before our marriage, my sister was tragically killed in a car accident. Two years after our marriage, my mother nearly died in another car accident. If obedience was the answer, why did these things happen to our family? Deciding there must not be a God after all, I turned my back on the faith of my youth.

In my weakness and vulnerability, I was lured by a man who would then betray me.

I am in no way excusing my behavior, or making myself out as some sort of martyr or victim, but simply a human being making choices in this world.

Through wrong choices and tragic circumstances beyond my control I developed fears, guilt, shame and feelings of unworthiness. I found myself being used, abused, berated, belittled and bewildered. I was like a prize fighter who gets knocked down and gets back up only to be knocked down again. I was on a merry-go-round of abuse and couldn't get off.

In 1994 I married the man I am married to today.

310

Life is not without its challenges, but now I turn toward God, not away.

I found a good Bible believing church near my home. I began praying that God would help me walk by the fruit of the spirit; love, joy, peace, patience, kindness, goodness, faithfulness, gentleness and self-control and not by the acts of the flesh; immorality, impurity, debauchery, idolatry, witchcraft, hatred, discord, jealousy, fits of rage, selfish ambition, dissentions, factions and envy, drunkenness, orgies and the like.

Most importantly, I have forgiven myself. This had the strongest hold on me until one day at Bible study a wise older woman asked, "Do you think God has forgiven you?"

"Yes, but I can't forgive myself."

"So, you think you're more important than God?"

My desire in sharing this, is for someone else who is lost, existing in a life of quiet desperation and no hope, to be set free. I want to help others find what I have found.

I longed for true peace of mind, true joy, true happiness and hope for the future and found it by running to God not away from God.

I have been touched by the Holy Spirit and know He dwells within me. I want others to know that God is there for them, if only they will reach out and trust. He doesn't want to punish us for our sins, but to save us from our sins.

When my heart opened up to Gods love, grace and mercy I could face the truth of my life, repent of my actions and accept God's will for my life, resting in Him.

I still have human frailties and know that neither life, nor I can be perfect, but my trust is in God. He is in charge. My job is to obey, let go and let God.

ACKNOWLEDGEMENTS

From the moment I met Rhonda Hayes Curtis, as a student in her "Write Your Own Story" class, I knew she was special. This book would not exist today without her. She went above and beyond the call of duty to help me every step of the way.

Her professionalism, compassion and perseverance kept me going when I wanted to give up. She is truly my angel and I will be forever grateful, not only for her mentoring, but also for her friendship.

I also want to thank my children, Tracy, Melissa, Becky and Chris for their unconditional love, giving me the freedom to tell my story.

Thank you also to my husband, Glenn, for his patience in allowing me the time it has taken to complete this task.

Finally, I want to thank God for his grace, mercy and love and for compelling me to write my story.

Made in the USA
San Bernardino, CA
01 February 2020